Praise for *Educating Ruby*

It was a teacher that changed my life; not because he taught me my times tables but because he helped me rebuild my confidence through my parents' divorce. I am Ruby, you are Ruby, we are all Ruby. Thank you Guy Claxton and Bill Lucas for breaking us out of the battery farm.

Richard Gerver, author of
Creating Tomorrow's Schools Today

Good schools have always focused on 'results plus', helping children achieve their potential in examinations and at the same time developing confident and creative individuals who are keen to do their very best. Guy Claxton and Bill Lucas are absolutely right to remind us of the need for more expansive approaches. *Educating Ruby* is a timely reminder of how increasingly important it is not to focus on just part of what matters at school.

Brian Lightman, General Secretary, ASCL

It is essential that schools educate the whole child. I strongly support the line of argument made by Bill Lucas and Guy Claxton that schools are about so much more than examination results. *Educating Ruby* is essential reading for everyone who cares about the future of education in our country.

Tony Little, Head Master, Eton College

D0185332

The UK school system is in urgent need of reform. *Educating Ruby* teems with practical, evidence-based, inspiring ideas for teaching and learning, that will brighten the lives of over-tested students, stressed-out teachers and concerned parents. And when politicians are finally ready to be pointed in the right direction, it's just the book for them too.

**Sue Palmer, literacy specialist
and author of *Toxic Childhood***

A powerful, heartfelt and expert analysis of what's going wrong in the education of our children and how to put it right.

Sir Ken Robinson

Examination grades are important, but they are only half the story of education. Parents send their children to schools like my own because they know we build the kinds of character and roundedness that this book puts its finger on. It's what all schools everywhere should be doing. Guy Claxton and Bill Lucas speak for schoolchildren and their parents everywhere.

Sir Anthony Seldon, Master, Wellington College

The need for a knowledge-rich curriculum is beyond dispute but this provocative book should make all teachers and school leaders think deeply about what is taught and how. A broad range of ideas encompassing deep scholarship, character building and creativity are set out with passion and clarity including practical suggestions for schools and parents. It's going to wind some people up – but that's a good thing.

**Tom Sherrington, Head Teacher,
Highbury Grove School**

The schools of tomorrow are here today – but are too few and far between. We won't get the speed and scale of change without real political will which is currently lacking. *Educating Ruby* is a brave attempt to mobilise parent power to get that change to happen. I really hope it succeeds!

Matthew Taylor, Chief Executive, RSA

Most people believe schools should do their bit to help children become 'rounded individuals' as well as developing their intellectual strength. The obsession with measuring our schools through testing their pupils means that too many children are on a relentless treadmill which is self-defeating. Ruby and her friends need an education with all its richness, with teachers who bring learning alive and supported by parents who play their full part. It is not too complicated and *Educating Ruby* explains why the system needs to change and what everyone can do about it.

Mick Waters, Professor of Education,
Wolverhampton University

What would schools look like if they taught children what they really need to know? Could we ever have schools like that? *Educating Ruby* is thoughtful, provocative and optimistic. As ever, Guy Claxton and Bill Lucas are wise and experienced voices on the cutting edge of education. All teachers and parents should read this book – they'd learn lots, and enjoy it!

Hilary Wilce, author of *Backbone: How to Build*
the Character Your Child Needs to Succeed

Educating Ruby is a must read book for all stakeholders in education. Guy Claxton and Bill Lucas show how we can have happy, positive young people with skills, attitudes and 'habits of mind'; who are knowledgeable *and* capable of passing examinations.

Sue Williamson, Chief Executive, SSAT

Whether you agree or disagree with *Educating Ruby*, you'll certainly be engaged, stimulated and challenged.

**Robert Wilne, founding Head Master,
London Academy of Excellence**

Tired of the endless false dichotomy presented by those with an interest in promoting 'solid, traditional' teaching methods above a 'progressive, airy-fairy' approach – or vice versa – Bill Lucas and Guy Claxton here point out, with optimism alongside experience, that there is a third option. *Educating Ruby* paints a picture of what an excellent education might look like in our modern world, and draws not only on what could be done, but what is actually happening in classrooms throughout the country today, to make the image both vivid and detailed. The authors feel strongly that there are skills and qualities we should be nurturing in our young people that cannot be tested by formal examination, but are nonetheless vital for a successful and happy adult life – and they ask some challenging, and potentially controversial questions – about the role of Big Data in true accountability. This is an accomplished and uplifting work; likely to leave the reader feeling considerably more empowered than oppressed.

Teach Secondary

Guy Claxton
Bill Lucas

with forewords by Professor Tanya Byron and Octavius Black

Educating
Ruby

what our children really need to learn

Crown House Publishing Limited
www.crownhouse.co.uk

First published by

Crown House Publishing
Crown Buildings, Bancyfelin, Carmarthen, Wales, SA33 5ND, UK
www.crownhouse.co.uk

and

Crown House Publishing Company LLC
6 Trowbridge Drive, Suite 5, Bethel, CT 06801-2858, USA
www.crownhousepublishing.com

First published 2015. Reprinted 2015 (twice), 2016 (twice).

British Library of Cataloguing-in-Publication Data

A catalogue entry for this book is available from the British Library.

Print ISBN 978-184590954-3
Mobi ISBN 978-184590970-3
ePub ISBN 978-184590971-0
ePDF ISBN 978-184590972-7

LCCN 2015935353

Printed and bound in the UK by
Gomer Press, Llandysul, Ceredigion

Acknowledgements

Thanks to:

Kayla Cohen, Bryan Harrison, Tom Middlehurst and Hilary Mackay Martin.

All those who spoke to us so openly about their own or their child's experiences of school.

The many head teachers and teachers with whom we are lucky to work, who are already putting these kinds of ideas into practice.

Our gurus: Professors Art Costa, David Perkins, Howard Gardner, Tanya Byron and Carol Dweck.

And our families: Henrietta, Jude, Tom, Bryony and Peter.

Contents

Foreword by
Professor Tanya Byron

I struggled at school. It was a highly academic girls' school, and its hot-house atmosphere didn't suit me. At one teachers' meeting, my parents and I were told, "Tanya will never be a high-flyer."

Jo Malone, the multi-millionaire businesswoman and fragrance queen, was told by a teacher that she was lazy (Jo is dyslexic) and "would never make anything of her life". Albert Einstein, Thomas Edison and thousands of others were written off by their teachers – because their way of learning didn't fit that of the school.

As a clinical psychologist working in child and adolescent mental health, I often meet children and young people who are struggling at school to such a degree that it has severely compromised their mental health and daily functioning. There are thousands of children today who are showing increasing rates of depression and anxiety disorders, struggling to hold on to a positive sense of self-worth. Some literally give up. And their parents are at their wits' end wondering what to do for the best.

While the mental health of our young is a complex, multifaceted issue driven by biological, psychological and social factors, I believe that the current education system is out of date and out of step with the learning needs and habits of young people. Some 50% of all adult mental health problems start at the age of 14, a time of life when the prefrontal cortex undergoes huge changes in function, when risk-taking is a developmental imperative on the road to individuation, and when puberty adds sexual, social and identity challenges. Children who struggle are not lazy, stupid or babyish; they just don't fit with this antiquated system.

School should foster a love of learning and enquiry, a thirst to discover and uncover, a sense of fun and creativity, whether learning about the past or developing ideas for the future. Yet many academics, like myself, who work in the fields of child development, education and mental health are increasingly concerned. We are deeply worried that our young people are being force-fed, over-tested and misunderstood, and are suffering as a result. They are taught to pass exams but not necessarily taught to think in their own unique way and on their own terms.

Our digitally literate and highly curious young people sit in classrooms where learning is delivered in ways that do not connect with the ways they think, learn and create. Furthermore, children from disadvantaged backgrounds, those with learning difficulties, or simply idiosyncratic learning styles, are never going to leave school feeling successful and empowered to carry on learning and thinking for themselves. This is not 'trendy sentiment', as some would have us believe, but a matter of hard fact. Those of us who have raised these concerns have been called 'The Blob' by policy-makers and politicians, and the hostility that exists between them and teachers is at an all-time high.

Recent surveys by employers and higher education institutions in the UK have clearly shown that students are not well-prepared for the transition from secondary education to higher education and/or employment. Children and young people are being educated to become reliable employees, when what we need are creative thinkers and problem-solvers.

The CBI's *First Steps* report describes British schools as grim exam factories where "while average performance rises gently, too many are left behind". It describes the education system as "too much of a conveyor belt – it moves children along at a certain pace, but does not deal well with individual needs ... [This] means we fail to properly stretch the able, while results for young people from disadvantaged backgrounds are particularly troubling." Their report says that there should be a major focus on cultivating the skills young people need in life.

So what are these skills?

Professors Guy Claxton and Bill Lucas are world-renowned academics who have dedicated their professional lives to answering this question. Their Building Learning Power programme is about helping young people to become more confident and sophisticated learners, both in school and out. Schools around the world – from Poland to Patagonia, from Manchester to Melbourne – are using these smart, practical ideas to give children the knowledge and the confidence they need to learn and thrive in the exciting and turbulent waters of the 21st century.

Guy and Bill have shown that it is perfectly possible for schools to systematically cultivate the habits of mind that enable young people to face all kinds of difficulty and uncertainty calmly, confidently and creatively. Students who are more confident of their own learning ability learn faster and learn better. They also do better in their tests and external examinations, and they are easier and more satisfying to teach.

It's not either/or – either good grades or life skills. We have to go beyond the weary old Punch and Judy battle between 'traditionalists' and 'progressives'. Children and young people who are helped to become more confident and powerful learners are happier, more adventurous and take greater pleasure in reading – and they do better on the tests.

To thrive in the 21st century, it is not enough to leave school with a clutch of examination certificates. Students need to have learned how to be tenacious and resourceful, imaginative and logical, self-disciplined and self-aware, collaborative and inquisitive. Bill and Guy's earlier book, *Expansive Education: Teaching Learners for the Real World*, gives dozens of examples of schools around the world that are already achieving this holy grail of education.

We need a radical rethink of our school systems to help our children get ready for the challenges and opportunities they will face. Without this equipment, many will flounder and become unhappy. But we can't wait for the politicians and policy-makers – they will always do too little, too late. Teachers and parents have to help each other to regenerate what goes on in schools via an alliance and a quiet revolution.

This book provides a rallying call for that vital alliance, and a manifesto for the evolution that has to come. Please read it, join the alliance and give copies to your friends.

Professor Tanya Byron,
Consultant in Child and Adolescent Mental Health,
Professor in the Public Understanding of Science

Foreword by
Octavius Black

I have a 4-year-old daughter. She is the smartest, sweetest, most delightful girl in the world ever. Honestly, she really is. Her mother and I are in no doubt. However, as important as what we think of our daughter today is what we want for her in the future.

In less than 20 years, the smartphone will have gone from being an exotic luxury to being the prized possession of 80% of the world's population. It will transform whole industries, wealth distribution and ways of life. As I write, the livelihood of iconic London taxi drivers is being put in jeopardy by the Uber app, which may in turn be transformed in a few years by the widespread adoption of driverless cars.

We hope that our daughter will live for another 90 years. Much of the knowledge she acquires at school is likely to be redundant by the time she starts her first job. Far more important to her working life will be the ability to read the runes and respond healthily to whatever challenges come her way. If she is curious, open minded and has grit she is far more likely to achieve the career objectives she sets herself than merely securing an A* in French. Education needs to instil a love of learning and the confidence to adapt and grow.

But work is only one small part of what will determine the quality of her life. Will she form healthy, romantic relationships? Will she suffer from mood disorder (the most susceptible group of children are teenage girls in social groups one and two, which will include her)? How will she respond to rejection and exclusion when, inevitably, she experiences them?

Our nation's leaders are responsible for building a workforce with the skills to secure good jobs and maintain the prosperity of our nation. As a citizen, I expect nothing less. But, as a parent, what matters most to me is that my daughter feels good about who she is, come what may: that she is psychologically healthy and robust. The primary duty for this falls with us, her parents. The science shows emphatically that how we talk with, respond to, set boundaries for and play alongside our children has the greatest impact on their emotional and psychological well-being. This is a responsibility we can all embrace.

But we also need to know that our schools are playing their part. That's difficult. Heads may not see it as their responsibility to build character, and may not know how. Harried teachers are likely to focus on exam results and Ofsted inspections. To help my daughter develop the traits she will need, schools need ideas, support and a bit of pressure. If we want to give our daughters and sons the best chance in life we need to work with their schools' governors, teachers and heads.

Professors Claxton and Lucas have given us this invaluable guide as to how to help, based not just on what we should do but also brimming with practical tools, techniques and examples on how to do it. As a parent, I'm immensely grateful. Once you have read this book, I suspect you will be too.

**Octavius Black, Co-founder and CEO of the
Mind Gym and Parent Gym**

Chapter 1

Causes for concern

I didn't understand what school was for. A lot of the teachers thought I was thick. I remember the head teacher saying I'd never make anything of myself in front of the whole school. My ability to learn in school had been pretty much crushed out of me quite young. I still feel scared when I hear that word, 'thick'.

Jack Dee, comedian

What we want for our children

We talk to lots of people about schools – teachers, parents, children and many others – and we think we have a shrewd idea about what is on people's minds. So here is what we are assuming about you, our readers. We know that you want the best for your children – your own and the ones you may teach. We think that means, roughly, that you want them to be happy, to lead lives that are rich and fulfilling, to grow up to be kind and loving partners and loyal friends, and to be free from poverty and fear. We assume this means having a job that is satisfying and makes a decent living. We guess you don't want your children to be as rich as Croesus if that brings with it being miserable, greedy or anxious.

We also suspect that you did not decide to have a child so that they could contribute to the economic prosperity of the country and become 'productive members of a world-class workforce'. We don't imagine that you think about your son or daughter, or the children you teach, as if they were pawns in a national economic policy or in a sociological quest for equity or upward mobility. (We reckon that you know people, as we do, who have real doubts about the idea that the more you make and spend the happier you will be, and who may even have down-sized in order to live in a way that feels more worthwhile or morally satisfying. There are plenty of happy plumbers with good degrees these days.)

And we assume that you would like your child's school to support you in those general aims. The aims of school do have to be general because we just can't know what kind of work and lifestyle will 'deliver' that quality of life for any individual. Children's lives will take many twists and turns, as yours and ours have, and whether they turn out to be accountants in Auckland, teachers in Namibia or shepherd-esses in Yorkshire, we will want them to have the same general qualities of cheerfulness, kindness, open-mindedness and fulfilment, won't we? (Please insert your own favourite words to describe those deepest wishes for your children here.)

We suspect that you might still be touched, as we are, by these words on children from Khalil Gibran's book *The Prophet* (much quoted though they may be):

2

Your children are not *your* children.

They are the sons and daughters of Life's longing for itself.

They come through you but not from you,

And though they are with you yet they belong not to you.

You may give them your love but not your thoughts,

For they have their own thoughts.

You may house their bodies but not their souls,

For their souls dwell in the house of tomorrow,

Which you cannot visit, not even in your dreams.

You may strive to be like them,

But seek not to make them like you.

For life goes not backward nor tarries with yesterday.[1]

If your household is full of 'digital natives', doing all kinds of wonderful and scary things on social and digital media – or you have ever watched a TV show called *Outnumbered* – you will be in no doubt that "their souls dwell in the house of tomorrow"! A mutual friend of ours was telling us, just the other day, about a conversation with his granddaughter, Edie, who is 12. She was doing something with her mobile phone and Martin asked her what it was. She showed him the app she had discovered for learning Japanese, which she had decided she would teach herself. Often in bed at night she would be listening and practising quietly, under the

1   Khalil Gibran, On Children, in *The Prophet* (New York: Alfred A. Knopf, 1923).

bedclothes. Her parents hadn't a clue what she was up to – she had not felt the need to tell them – and her teachers, earnestly trying to get her to write small essays on 'the functions of the computer mouse', certainly had no idea. Will Edie be working in the Tokyo branch of Ernst & Young in 15 years' time? Who knows.

We make the assumption that you are doing your best to help your children get ready for whatever comes along, both at home and at school, and preferably both together. If you have children of your own at school, we assume you would like the school to be your partner in this crucial enterprise. And if you are a teacher, we assume that you take immense pride in the amazing job you have: helping to launch the lives of hundreds of children in the best way you know how. We are all angling the launch pad, so to speak, so that – whatever they are going to be – they get the best possible send-off. Whether you are helping little ones learn how to tell the time and 'play nicely', or bright 17-year-olds to grapple with A level English or the International Baccalaureate's theory of knowledge module, we'll assume you don't want to take your eye off that fundamental intention of getting them ready for life. What could possibly be a more fulfilling way of earning a living?

All is not well

However, we are also going to imagine that you, like us, have some serious misgivings about what is actually happening in schools. In the boxes scattered throughout the next few pages, and later in the book, there are some stories and quotations from children, their parents and teachers. We've put them there to see if you share some of the same feelings and experiences. The schools and the people we talked to are all real but, in most cases, we've changed or removed their names to protect their anonymity.

I'd loved my primary school, but at St Bede's Comprehensive School I felt depressed and scared, like a wild animal in a cage. I felt empty inside. I was ill once for two weeks, I felt wiped out and tired; but mentally I felt happy because of not being at school. When I returned, however, after just one day I came home and felt restless, confused, my mind couldn't focus on one thing at a time. I felt unsettled and one tiny thing would make me flip into tears.

If ever the teacher was challenged by a pupil about what they said, the pupil would get told off. I got told off for telling the teacher that a boy was teasing me by saying he liked to kill animals, when we were on the subject of animal cruelty. She said to me, "Now that was a *stupid* thing to say wasn't it?" – what I'd said, not the boy. I looked at her – why in the world would that be stupid? I raised my hand again. I wanted to say something that sounded strong. But when she said, "Have you got some-thing *sensible* to say now?" I felt the gaze of all my classmates on my back, and I lost my nerve as tears filled my eyes and clogged my throat. "No," I said.

I felt resentful but couldn't bring myself to become a rebel. So I became quiet and my normal self was glazed over by someone different – who I didn't like. There was no room at St Bede's for someone different like me. And I felt myself turning into some fashion freak like

5

everyone else. I hated it because keeping my feelings to myself is very hard. Because normally they're very strong. I was always hiding myself while I battled through the day.

I had to let my feelings out, but I couldn't wait to tell mum at the end of the day, so I turned to my friend Leanne who was good at talking about sensitive subjects. When I did she would always try to help me fix them – until one day she said, "Look, Annie, I know you're not enjoying it, but I am and I don't really want to talk about it because it's not positive." Then I had no one to talk to.

That was another thing about St Bede's. You were told to "Stop being childish", but we *were* children so we *had* to be childish! We weren't allowed to run about at break-time. This was one of the things I found utterly stupid. There was a boy in my class that was always bouncing in his seat and shouting out because of this. He had never been like that before [at primary school].

Annie, Year 7 student,
St Bede's Comprehensive School

What are your concerns about the schooling you are providing (if you are a teacher) or your child is getting (if you are a parent)? Of course, many children thrive in school, if they are lucky enough to find one that suits them. They retain their cheerfulness and gentleness, enjoy maths and English, find a sport and a musical instrument they love to play and practice, and are helped to discover and explore the interests and aptitudes that may grow into the basis of a degree and a career. (Though even conspicuous successes like Tom, on page 8, can have their misgivings.)

But many don't. A lot of parents and teachers see their 'bright' children becoming anxiously fixated on grades and losing the adventurous, enquiring spirit they had when they were small. They study because 'it is going to be on the test', not because it is interesting or useful. Or adults see their 'less able' children (we'll query this kind of terminology later on) becoming ashamed of their constant inability to do what is required, and so becoming either actively resistant to school or passive and invisible. Both ends of the achievement spectrum can experience a curious but intense mixture of stress and boredom. The obsession with grades and test scores turns some children into conservative and docile 'winners' at the examination game. Many muddle by in the middle, willing to play a game they don't fully understand.

And some children grow into defeated 'losers'. Yet these losers (like the talented Jack Dee) are not inherently stupid or lazy. Research shows that they have the potential for highly intelligent and determined problem-solving in real-life settings, but some of them, tragically, have had the learning stuffing knocked out of them by their experience at school, and as a result they are less happy, less creative and less successful than they could be. That is not giving them the best, and it is not nurturing the talent and the grit that would help them to be happy people and thoughtful citizens. Many people's concerns about school centre on the validity of the examination system, and on the effect that the focus on tests and exams had on them or is having on their children.

For many young people the stressful nature of school is compounded by the sheer pointlessness of much of what they are expected to learn. It is a rare parent (or teacher) who is able to come up with a convincing reason why every 15-year-old needs to know the difference between metamorphic and igneous rocks or to explain the subplots in *Othello*. Parents often find themselves trapped in a conflict between sympathising with their children about the apparent irrelevance of much of the curriculum and still trying to make them study it. Certainly up to GCSE there is a fear that, if children don't do their best to knuckle down and 'get the grades', their life choices will be forever narrowed and blighted. And, under the present antiquated system, they are quite right to be concerned. The horns of this particular dilemma are sharp and painful.

Teachers may have other quandaries – for example, wanting to impart to their students their own love of reading and literature, and knowing, from bitter experience, that the effect on many 15-year-olds of having to study *The Tempest* or *Jane Eyre* is exactly the opposite. Not everyone is brave (or foolish) enough to be the charismatic, rebellious Robin Williams character (John Keating) from *Dead Poets Society*, or Hector (Richard Griffiths) from *The History Boys*. Politicians who blithely tinker with the set books rarely spend longer in a school than it takes for the photo opportunity to be secured, so have no conception of the damage and distress their doctrinaire beliefs and prejudices may be causing. Many teachers are caught between the rock of their own values and passions and the hard place of examination requirements.

My school gave me a great education really. I gained good GCSEs and A levels. I was always involved in the school plays and drama competitions, winning several times. I took part in a host of extra-curricular activities and, as head boy, I had opportunities to speak publically on local, national and international platforms. Yet when

I arrived at Oxford, I found myself shying away from the drama societies, the debates and even whole-hearted participation in my course – things that I would have loved and done naturally at school. What was missing? Why did my outlook change so drastically?

I think it was because, as a 'gifted' student, I was constantly protected from risk. Academic learning came naturally to me, so I never experienced real difficulty and was allowed to glide happily and successfully through school. Although excellent in many ways, my education allowed me – almost encouraged me – to develop an aversion to risk and failure. To this day I still cannot ride a bike. As a child I tried once – I fell off, it hurt – and I didn't see the point of getting on again. I still stubbornly refuse to learn about car maintenance and electrics, and anything else I see as outside my realms of understanding. How different my life might have been if my school (as many now do) had deliberately nurtured an appetite for adventure and a tolerance for error!

Of course, young people need knowledge: no one is arguing against that. But they need more – they need the habits of mind that will allow them to become adaptive, responsive and caring people. And, as educators, I now see that we have the power to help them with this – or to hinder them completely.

**Tom Middlehurst,
head of research at SSAT (The Schools Network)**

For Tom there is a real feeling of having been rendered conservative and brittle by his, apparently successful, education. It was the same for Bill who went to Oxford to study English literature, where he discovered he had been taught how to outwit the A level examiner rather than to work his way into a difficult novel or poem and then articulate his *own* opinions.

For other people (like Annie's mum, who sent us her daughter's sad reflections) their worries are more about a school culture that is callous or indifferent to their children's feelings, interests and anxieties. It's no use telling Annie to 'buck up' and 'stop being babyish'. She has a perfect right to her own, rather mature, concerns about animal cruelty. If she is being told to 'toughen up', and to deny her own moral sensibilities, then her teacher is unreasonably taking sides in a serious ethical debate, and Annie is being told that her qualms and reactions are invalid. Many parents see their kind, sensitive children being brutalised by the culture of school. Bullying does not need to be overt and physical, although it often is. Children can be very unkind and cliquish, and it is the job of adults to moderate those effects. Annie certainly should not feel she has to become a "fashion freak" in order to have any friends. She *is* trying to toughen up and hold her ground, but when you are 11 you can do with some support.

Annie was lucky not to go down the same route as Chloe who started self-harming when she was just 12 as a way of coping with being unhappy at school. In an interview in *The Independent* in October 2013, Chloe says, "One day in class I dug my nails into my arm to stop me crying, and I was surprised by how much the physical pain distracted me from the emotional pain. Before long I was regularly scratching myself, deeper each time." In 2012–2013, over 5,000 10 to 14-year-olds were treated by the NHS for self-harm, a rise of 20% on the previous year. Many of their worries stemmed from school.[2]

Here are another couple of experiences.

My daughter was like some spirally shape that was being pushed into a square box, and it was soul destroying. I'd take this gorgeous little girl to school, and then I'd pick up this really deflated person. She's quite creative and dreamy. She'd look out the window, see a cloud and make up a story, but the teachers would shout at her to focus on her work … She became more insecure, more deflated, she cried more. She'd always been a good sleeper – she started waking at night. She became much less confident. She gets so over-tired by the workload that she kind of zones out. So she's not having much happy awake time … and that's no way to live.

**Sandy, mother of a child now
in a London secondary school**

As a parent you want your child to feel happy, safe emotionally, to enjoy themselves. When you see your child going into negative spirals, it is highly exhausting … What really did it for me was when she was looking out of the window, looking devastated, and she saw a rock that had cracked, and she said, "That's how I feel; I'm broken inside."

**Pippa, mother of a Year 5 girl
in a London primary school**

2   Kate Hilpern, Why do children self-harm?, *The Independent* (8 October 2013). Available at: http://www.independent.co.uk/life-style/health-and-families/features/why-do-so-many-children-selfharm-8864861.html.

Some other views

School leavers 'unable to function in the workplace'

More than four in 10 employers are being forced to provide remedial training in English, maths and IT amid concerns teenagers are leaving school lacking basic skills, it emerged today.[3]

It's not just parents (and many teachers) who are unhappy with the schooling system. Variants of the headline above can be found in many British newspapers today as employers find that the 'residues' with which young people emerge from school at 16 or 19 do not include the necessary basic skills to cope in the workplace. In 2012, the employers' organisation, the Confederation of British Industry (CBI), produced a thoughtful report, *First Steps: A New Approach For Our Schools*. In it they articulate two strong arguments.

The first calls for the development of a clear, widely owned and stable statement of the outcomes that all schools are committed to delivering. These, the report argues, should "go beyond the merely academic, into the behaviours and attitudes schools should foster in everything they do".[4] This statement should be the benchmark against which we judge all new policy ideas, schools and the structures we set

---

3 Graeme Paton, School leavers 'unable to function in the workplace', *The Telegraph* (11 June 2012). Available at: http://www.telegraph.co.uk/education/educationnews/9322525/School-leavers-unable-to-function-in-the-workplace.html.

4 CBI, *First Steps: A New Approach For Our Schools* (London: CBI, 2012). Available at: http://www.cbi.org.uk/media/1845483/cbi_education_report_191112.pdf.

up to monitor them. Are there good reasons for supposing that these modifications will enhance the desired outcomes? If not, go back to the drawing board. The report notes that "in the UK we have often set out aspirational goals [for education] … but we have rarely been clear about how the system will deliver them", or about how they are to be assessed. "[D]elivery has been judged by an institutional measure – exam results – that is often not well linked to the goals set out at the political level."[5]

The second concern in *First Steps* is the conspicuous lack of engagement by parents and the wider community in schooling. If parents do not feel that they are involved in a partnership with a school that has their child's best interests at heart, or are not confident that they have a shared understanding of what those best interests are, children's education is bound to suffer. Professor John Hattie's research, which the report quotes, has shown that "the effect of parental engagement over a student's school career is equivalent to adding an extra two to three years to that student's education".[6] There is a consequent call for the adoption by schools of a strategy for fostering parental engagement and wider community involvement, including links with business. We'll go more deeply into the CBI's thoughtful argument about how schools need to change in Chapter 5.

It is worth noting that this call for schools to do more in the way of developing habits and attitudes, and engaging with communities, is not coming from fringe groups of 'swivel-eyed loons' or 'bleeding-heart liberals'. It is coming from one of the most hard-nosed, well-informed organisations in British culture. They are certainly not members of

---

5   CBI, *First Steps*.
6   John Hattie, *Visible Learning: A Synthesis of Over 800 Meta-Analyses Relating to Achievement* (London: Routledge, 2008).

what previous Secretary of State for Education Michael Gove so dismissively referred to as 'The Blob' – a hundred senior education scholars who have devoted much of their lives to trying to understand and improve a really complex system rather than settling for simplistic and antiquated nostrums.

Indeed, within the professional circles of people who know and care about the state of our schools, there is almost universal concern – not because they are politically extreme in any direction but because they know, first hand, what a mixed blessing education can turn out to be. Many school leaders, for example, are not happy with the status quo. Two current campaigns are illustrative of this. The first is called the Great Education Debate, led by one of the two main head teacher professional associations, the Association of School and College Leaders (ASCL). The other is called Redesigning Schooling, led by The Schools Network (the organisation of which Tom Middlehurst is director of research). We explore these ideas in more detail in Chapter 5. You can decide for yourselves whether what they are saying mirrors your own concerns.

University departments and colleges of education are full of people trying to improve the lot of your children. Of course, some of them may have strange or radical ideas about what this means, but many are serious scholars who try to see more deeply, and read the evidence more dispassionately, than politicians and journalists are prone to do.

John Hattie has recently been hugely successful at making complex research accessible to teachers. This has been achieved partly through his painstaking analysis of the research, partly by lucid writing, and especially by using simple 'dashboard' images, like the one opposite, which make it very easy to compare the size of the effect that different teaching methods have on students' examination performance. (Statistically, any effect size above 0.4 on the scale is worth having. Below that, the benefits for students' achievements are trivial or even sometimes negative.)

Understanding effect sizes

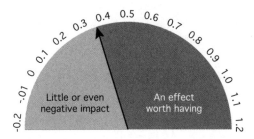

His work has generated some surprises. According to the research, grouping students by 'ability' – the kind of setting that traditionalists like so much – has an effect size of just 0.12.[7] Top sets benefit a little, while lower sets do worse than they would if they had not been segregated. If you care about everyone, not just the designated 'winners', this is an inconvenient truth. Reducing class sizes from 30 to 20 has almost no effect – and it is very expensive – unless, that is, you take this reduction as an opportunity to teach in a different way. Carry on teaching the 20 in the same way you taught the 30 and you might just as well set fire to a big pile of £20 notes. It is the nature of teaching itself that makes the big difference, not tinkering with structural features like the way children are batched, but you would never learn

---

7 See Hattie, *Visible Learning.*

that from most of what passes for debate in the media and in parliament.

Some common issues

There are a wide variety of issues that concern parents, educators and employers more broadly. In different ways, and with different emphases, parents and employers share a host of concerns about the big issues besetting us today, many of which raise questions about education. These include such questions as:

- If the internet is both a force for good and for innovation, and an unreliable source of information and fraught with opportunities for cyber-bullying, how should we regulate and educate young people to be both safe and adventurous?

- Do we have to accept that the decline of reading for pleasure is the result of living in an e-world? How should schools balance surfing and gaming with the encouragement to get lost for hours in a gripping book?

- Are children, at root, 'little savages', inherently naughty and lazy, as some of the Victorians believed, who just have to be trained and disciplined, made to do boring and difficult things that seem pointless, and punished if they don't comply 'for their own good', in order to civilise them? Or do they learn self-control better in other, less draconian, ways?

- How can we promote religious tolerance in an increasingly war-scarred world? What can schools do to immunise young people against the torrent of violent propaganda they can find on the web at a click of a mouse?

● Is climate change an inconvenient fact requiring us to change our habits, or an example of bad science? Is fiddling around trying to 'balance' chemical equations a necessary preliminary to engaging with this question, or a distraction?

There is a huge amount of discussion and debate about education these days. Much of it quickly gets technical and statistical and becomes hard to follow; and much of it is fuelled by passionately held beliefs, largely based on 'what worked (or didn't work) for me', generating more heat than light. We all have views because we all went to school, so we think we are experts on the topic. We are all – or nearly all – honourable, well-meaning people who wish the best for the children in our care. But we can't all be right. Should we go back to the past, to strict discipline and three-hour written exams, to hard subjects like Latin and algebra that train children's minds in the arts of rationality and retention? Or should we push on to a new future of demanding project work and self-expression, collaboration and problem-solving, continuous assessment and portfolios?

Both of us remember at school having to learn a long poem by Macaulay about a battle for a Roman bridge. One stanza went:

Those behind cried "Forward!"
And those before cried "Back!"
And backward now and forward
Wavers the deep array;
And on the tossing sea of steel,

To and fro the standards reel;
And the victorious trumpet-peal
Dies fitfully away.

It feels like that in the battle for education at the moment. Let's take a closer look at what the battling forces believe: what is inscribed on their different 'standards'.

Chapter 2

Why old school won't work

Education is an admirable thing, but it is well to remember from time to time that nothing that is worth knowing can be taught.

Oscar Wilde

We start this chapter with a quick overview of the debate about education. The situation is confused, and the picture we'll present is somewhat oversimplified, but we hope it will help you get oriented for when you get into more detailed discussions about school. In the public imagination there are, very roughly, three 'tribes' of educational opinion. They have different diagnoses of what is wrong with schools, and correspondingly three different sets of ideas about what needs doing to put it right. As we tend to meet these fairly frequently in the media, and in conversation, it's worth arming ourselves with some clarity about their strengths and weaknesses. Within each camp there are people who hold the most extreme views, and many more who subscribe to more moderate versions. It will quickly become clear which tribe we belong to, though we will try to do some justice to the other positions.

Three educational tribes: Roms, Trads and Mods

The first tribe we will call the Roms, short for romantics. The stereotype of the Roms is that they believe in the innate goodness of children, and therefore assume that education should allow children to express themselves and discover their own talents and interests. Didactic teaching and adult authority are seen as impositions that cramp and quite possibly damage this inherent spirit. The most extreme Roms have a deep trust, not borne out by evidence, that if children are just left alone, all will turn out for the best. (They've obviously never read *Lord of the Flies*.) The patron saint, as it were, of the Roms, is the 18th century French philosopher Jean-Jacques Rousseau who articulated this view in his didactic novel *Emile*. Famous exponents of the Rom philosophy include Rudolf Steiner (who did indeed have some fairly wacky ideas), Maria Montessori and, most notoriously, A. S. Neill of Summerhill. Real Roms tend to home-school their children or send them to small 'alternative' schools. The main characteristic of the Roms is that they are few and far between these days. There are almost none to be found in mainstream schools or in colleges of education.

The second tribe are the traditionalists, Trads for short. They tend to think that the ideal school is the good old-fashioned grammar school, with lots of chalk-and-talk teaching, strong discipline, conventional examinations (and plenty of them) and an emphasis in the curriculum on literacy, numeracy, timeless classics (Shakespeare, Beethoven) and difficult abstract subjects (grammar, algebra). To the Trads, teachers are respected sources of culturally important, tried and tested factual knowledge (the periodic table, the Tudors). Their job is to tell children about this knowledge and to make sure they have understood it well enough, and remembered it long enough, to pass exams in it.

These exams (especially A level) are vitally important and entirely fair and reliable, and they act as the gateways to the best universities (which, in turn, give access to well-paid professional jobs which will make you wealthy and therefore happy). After children have taken these exams, Trads seem to lose interest in the question of what this patchwork of factual knowledge actually enables children to do. It seems to them self-evident that mere acquaintance with facts is a good thing. Perhaps the implicitly valued capabilities are 'the ability to hold your own at dinner parties' and 'to do well on televised tests of general knowledge', such as *Who Wants to Be a Millionaire?*, *Mastermind*, *Eggheads* and especially *University Challenge*.

Trads believe that success in this educational obstacle race reflects the joint operation of a trio of entirely unproblematic factors: ability (which is fixed), hard work (which is under pupils' control) and good teaching by the school. (We'll come back to ability and effort shortly.) Trads believe that armies of Roms have for years been trying to take over the education system, and that all educational ills and disappointments of the last 50 years result from this infiltration. Any attempts to question this reassuringly straightforward picture is treated as 'progressive claptrap'.

Core to the Trads' world view is a belief that things can be divided neatly into twos, which means that anyone who isn't a Trad must be a Rom. But there is a third very important tribe of people who are signed up to neither traditional nor progressive views, but who are trying to think more carefully about how schools can best prepare children and young people – all of them – to flourish in the real, turbulent world of the mid 21st century. We'll call them the Mods, which is short for both modest and moderate. Mods know, when things are complicated, that patience and humility are required, and like the famous tortoise, they make, over time, better progress than the more doctrinaire hare.

Education is a prime example of a 'wicked' problem, one that is very complex and ill-defined, so Mods are painfully aware that quick fixes, appeals to nostalgia and rhetorical point-scoring don't cut it. They are much more at home with the kind of intelligence that the great psychologist Jean Piaget described as "knowing what to do when you don't know what to do". Mods become pensive, they tinker and explore, while the Trads get more pugnacious and the Roms disappear to the margins. Almost everyone who works in education is a Mod. But because Mods prefer to tinker quietly than to bang big drums, it is easy to underestimate how many there are, and how much progress teachers, head teachers and their schools have been making.

It is one of our ambitions for this book that we can create a more confident and more unified Mod voice with which to challenge the naive polarisations of the Roms and the Trads. As you will have guessed, we are Mods, and a good deal of our working year is spent with thousands of students, teachers, parents and employers who know we cannot turn the clock back to an allegedly 'golden age' of grammar schools, and nor can we make do with simplistic quick fixes. We have to think carefully, debate respectfully, experiment slowly and review honestly as we go along. In this way genuine progress will be made.

Trad beliefs

Because Trads tend to be loud and confident, there is a risk of being swept away by their rhetoric, especially when you are feeling confused by all the different claims and counter-claims. So we need to look a little more carefully at the case they make for going back to more traditional styles of education.

Sometimes Trads assume that, as well as being of unquestionable value in its own right, the mere possession of 'culturally valuable knowledge' somehow bestows on the owner an ability to think rationally. Traditionally this assumption applied to the ability to read and write Latin, and there are still those who champion Latin as the ultimate training of the mind. Currently ranked a very respectable 6,339 in the Amazon best-seller list, *Gwynne's Latin* claims, "What Latin, when taught in the traditional way, does is to train the learner's intellect and character as no other subject can even begin to do. It trains the learner to focus and concentrate; to memorise; to analyse, if necessary with minute exactness, and to problem-solve; to be diligent; to be conscientious; to be persevering; and much more. Learning Latin in the traditional manner makes us better at every human activity."[1] Now, we wholeheartedly agree with Mr Gwynne that the purpose of studying much of the syllabus

---

1   N. M. Gwynne, *Gwynne's Latin: The Ultimate Introduction to Latin Including the Latin in Everyday English* (London: Ebury Press, 2014).

is not to master the subject matter per se. Most of it will be of no use to the majority of those who struggle with it. We manage perfectly well without remembering the French imperfect tense or the equation for photosynthesis. Its main purpose is to develop useful, transferable qualities or 'habits of mind', such as concentration, perseverance and analytical precision. The trouble is, there is absolutely no evidence that Latin, when taught in the 'traditional way', has any such effect. The thinking you learn by studying Latin does not transfer to other subjects in the way it was imagined it might.[2]

More recently, such claims tend to be made for the study of mathematics, and now it seems to apply to any form of knowledge that a traditionally inclined secretary of state for education deems to be a 'cultural treasure'. Merely engaging with this subject matter in a way that enables you to recall it and manipulate it (in the highly prescribed ways required for exams) is thought to provide this training of the mind. But it doesn't. All the evidence shows that learning any particular thing, be it *Grand Theft Auto* or Latin, makes you better at that thing, but unless you are taught in a very particular way (more on this later), the benefits do not automatically transfer to any other domain. In fact, this is true for every subject on the secondary school curriculum. If taught in the traditional way, they do not make you any better at general-purpose thinking. Harvard Professor David Perkins wrote a very good empirical paper on this way back in 1985, called

---

2 Edward Thorndike was the first to discover the lack of transfer effect and a quick Google will show you many more contemporary studies in a similar vein.

'Post-primary education has little impact on informal reasoning', which about says it all.[3]

Curiously, despite their apparent belief in the possibility of such general mind training, Trads often argue, when it suits them, exactly the reverse. The explicit attempt to cultivate 'transferable thinking skills' is doomed, they say, because any method of thinking is so tightly bound to a particular subject matter that no such transfer is possible. The high priest of the Trads is a retired American professor called E. D. Hirsch, who keeps insisting that any direct attempt by teachers to cultivate mental abilities, such as précising material or distinguishing between the main message and more subordinate messages, is not only doomed to failure; it is the main reason why many poor children don't read very well and don't do well in exams. As far as we can tell, Hirsch's view is that simply *knowing* this venerable content – not being required to think about it, analyse it, distil it or use it to spark your imagination – somehow makes you an educated human being. We don't quite understand why being able to write an A grade essay on the symbolism in Wordsworth's poetry should make anyone a more competent and fulfilled human being. Throughout history, and across cultures, there seem to be a lot of people who have managed perfectly well without this particular accomplishment, and many others like them.

This emphasis on just knowing, and its associated feeling of being securely *right*, is deeply characteristic of Trads. They seem to greatly prefer knowing to thinking. They like to be certain, and to defend their certainty with any rhetorical tricks they can muster. Even though they hate to appear

---

3   David Perkins, Post-primary education has little impact on informal reasoning, *Journal of Educational Psychology* 77(5) (1985): 562–571.

ignorant of anything, they are often deeply confused about, for example, the difference between being knowledgeable, being clever and being genuinely intelligent. While these three states are clearly different, Trads often seem to think that not knowing something – being ignorant – is the same thing as being stupid, and that both are causes of shame. Some of them seem to like to catch people out – for example, by taking little quotes out of context and subjecting them to ridicule. They enjoy debating and winning arguments, and will deploy selective and distorted evidence when it suits them. Trads also confuse the ability to retain and retrieve knowledge with 'intelligence'. A definition of 'intelligence', endorsed by 52 leading experts in the field, specifically cautions: "Intelligence is not merely book learning, a narrow academic skill, or test-taking smarts. It reflects a broader and deeper capability for ... 'catching on', 'making sense' of things, and 'figuring out' what to do."[4]

It is perhaps not surprising that Trads are over-represented in the worlds of politics, the law and journalism, where skills in adversarial debating and point scoring are highly prized. Such sophistry is, of course, very different from real thinking, which is an often hesitant, difficult and slow attempt to get closer to the truth. Mods like to discuss and wonder, edging their way towards ideas that feel more solidly appropriate to the unprecedented challenges of the present.

* * *

Being busy defending an already espoused point of view leaves little time for real exploration. For example, Trads

---

4 Linda Gottfredson, Mainstream science on intelligence, *Wall Street Journal* (13 December 1994).

have tended to select the work of a few academics who support their case and ignore everything and everyone else. Two of the most revered and respectable American academics writing about the future of education are the co-founders of Harvard's influential Project Zero, Howard Gardner, and the man we mentioned a few paragraphs ago, David Perkins. You would have thought they would be worth a look, but they are never referred to by the Trads: they don't suit their case. As Trads tend to have exaggerated respect for 'top' universities, they can't rubbish the well-respected work of scholars like Perkins and Gardner, so they just pretend that they don't exist.

Likewise, a detailed, critical review of E. D. Hirsch's work by Kristen Buras in the *Harvard Educational Review*, in which she carefully rebuts all of Hirsh's claims, has gone unmentioned by many Trad defenders.[5] Hirsch says schools and teacher training have been 'taken over by progressive doctrine': they haven't. He says proper knowledge has been driven out of the curriculum: it hasn't. He says 'traditional subject matter' is beyond question: it isn't. He says the effort to memorise material produces understanding: it doesn't. He says you have to have memorised swathes of 'knowledge' before you can engage with it critically or creatively: you don't. And on it goes.

Because Trads like to keep things simple, they reduce knowledge to facts (and ignore the fact that most knowledge actually consists of webs of ideas that have withstood empirical tests). They reduce the subtle art of teaching to 'knowledge transmission' – just telling. They like to make assessment as rigorous as possible by making everything

---

5 Kristen Buras, Questioning core assumptions: a critical reading of and response to E. D. Hirsch's *The Schools We Need and Why We Don't Have Them* (essay review), *Harvard Educational Review* 69(1) (1999): 67–93.

right or wrong – which, of course, ignores thinking. And they have a simplistic view of students' minds which revolves around memorising: putting facts into storage and hauling them out on demand. This world view obliterates much of what is interesting and true about the mind as something which grapples with ideas, copes with degrees of uncertainty, interprets and muses – and sometimes improves – on what it has read or heard and, critically, is capable of getting better at grappling, interpreting, musing and, indeed, memorising.

Young minds are full of habits and processes that are capable of being stretched and strengthened by the right kind of teaching, but which are often not. A major study conducted by the Massachusetts Institute of Technology (MIT), Harvard and other partner universities found that students' performance on tests is powerfully predicted by their level of these mental skills and habits, but that studying in the traditional Hirschean way does not develop these skills.[6] They *can* be developed. It is extremely useful if they *are* developed. But, because this leads into slightly more complicated conceptualisations of young minds and how they may be taught, this possibility is often simply ignored or rubbished.

We have already noted Trads' tendency to reduce the multi-hued world to black and white. So, there is content – stuff to be learned and mastered – and then there is process – the way it is learned. Trads define them as separable and set them in opposition. So they wrongly conclude that, if you are interested in the processes and skills of thinking well, that must mean that you have stopped caring about

---

6 See Amy Finn, Matthew Kraft, Martin West et al., Cognitive skills, student achievement tests, and schools, *Psychological Science* 25(3) (2014): 736–744.

Shakespeare and algebra. This makes as much sense as saying that paying attention to the skill of hammering means that you no longer care where you are putting the nail. Duh!

Trads sometimes claim there are two kinds of people, novices and experts. Experts know enough to be able to think and solve problems. Novices don't, so they have to be filled up with facts before they become capable of thinking. Which means the attempt to get children wrestling with problems they are not yet 'expert' about is 'progressive nonsense'. But both understanding and skill grow precisely by working at the limit of what you currently can do or know. Knowledge is not like a pile of bricks which, when it becomes big enough, magically turns into a house; it is like a tree that grows by daring to put out shoots into the unknown. Put four 6-year-olds around an internet-enabled laptop, give them 45 minutes to find out as much as they can about a difficult question (What would happen if all the insects died? Why do people dance?) and just see how much they learn, and how they stretch their abilities as researchers. Any parent knows that children's most powerful learning tools are questioning and thinking, not memorising and regurgitating. Duh!

This apparent inability to count beyond two, and the consequent tendency to turn every issue, however complicated, into a Punch and Judy show, means that debate in education makes agonisingly slow progress when it is dominated by Trads. Although there are not very many of the most rabid Trads, they unfortunately make up for scarcity with volume. And they get in the way of precious, faltering attempts to think carefully about what a 21st century education could and should really be like.

Because they can only see in black and white, Trads try to persuade the world that all moderates are really romantics: that anyone who questions their regressive nostrums is a 'trendy liberal' who would turn all children into illiterate, uncultured savages. Academics like Robin Alexander at Cambridge or Andrew Pollard at Bristol, innovative head teachers like Sir Anthony Seldon at Wellington College or Tom Sherrington at Highbury Grove School in London, or thoughtful ex-teachers and administrators like Sir Tim Brighouse, who have spent decades thinking about schools and trying to improve them, are lumped together and treated like airheads. As we've said, some high-profile Trads have dubbed all academics who disagree with them 'The Blob'. They think millions of intelligent, well-informed teachers and parents are so gullible that they have become 'Prisoners of the Blob'.

Parents need a more honest and accurate picture of what the Mods are up to, and how their work over the last few decades, far from ruining schools, has been quietly laying the foundation for an education that is of real benefit to all young people (and not just the half that will go to university).

It's getting tedious. All this pressure around exams. A lot of my friends will cry about it. My friend was shouted at for getting an A, and was told that she needed to get an A* to be considered 'good enough'. I was told to drop art instead of history GCSE. They said that because art is not an academic subject you don't need it. It makes you feel really down and stressed about everything.

**Kirsty, Year 11, girls' grammar school,
south-west England**

I don't really get much benefit out of school. Until you can get your examination grades, there's literally nothing to show for your improvements and your efforts and your time. There's no satisfaction. The joy of learning dies down after six years and it gets a bit tedious.

Abedi, Year 11, London secondary school

Speaking up for the Mods

It is time, we think, to encourage teachers, parents, employers and children themselves to hold hands and speak up. Parents worry about exam stress and the loss of their children's joy in learning. Teachers know that controlling crowds of bored teenagers, or squeezing a few extra children across an arbitrary assessment borderline, is not what lights their fire. It is not why they wanted to become teachers in the first place. Employers know that being able to knock out an essay on the causes of the First World War or solve quadratic equations is no guarantee that youngsters are ready for the world of work. University admission tutors want to know if applicants can think on their feet, and not just trot out well-rehearsed answers to anticipated questions. And children themselves want to feel that what they are doing in school is really preparing them to be confident, capable, learning adults. All these causes for concern are deep and real and valid, and not to be pooh-poohed by those who cannot see beyond the status quo. Millions of us know that the examination game cannot be the be-all and end-all of education, that there has to be another way of 'winning' at school. This 'other game' is what we are going to describe in the coming chapters. It is about how we can help children and young people to get a really good start in life from their schooling even if they didn't do well on the tests. And it is about why high achievers need this other game just as much.

There may be a number of reasons why opposition to the Trads is not more vocal. Teachers need to know that their concerns and ideas are welcome in their staffrooms – but not all head teachers are ready to hear it. Parents may think it is 'just us' or 'just our family', without realising that dozens of people in the same street are dealing with very similar misgivings. They may not quite know how to put those feelings into words – parents are often intimidated by schools, especially if their own experience as a schoolchild was not happy or successful. Some parents may feel that school is more or less the way it has to be, and lack confidence in their ability to challenge and suggest. Some may be well aware of their and their children's concerns, but feel that they have no option – if they are to do their best for their children – but to tell them to knuckle down and 'suck it up'. To play the game as well as you can and hope to get a place at as good a university as possible seems like the only sound advice they can give, and so they stifle their doubts.

John Watts, a wise head teacher in the 1960s, said that "parents, however much they have suffered at school, or even if they left with a sense of failure, usually attribute the shortcomings to themselves rather than to the system, and thus find it difficult to envisage school in any form other than the one they themselves experienced".[7] So they sit on their hands.

---

7 John Watts, The changing role of the classroom teacher. In Clive Harber, Roland Meighan and Brian Roberts (eds), *Alternative Educational Futures* (London: Holt Education, 1984).

Exam fodder

There is another Trad myth that says that everyone can do well if they try hard enough – except, sadly, for those who, when the brains were being doled out, were at the end of the queue and got small ones. This means that, if you did poorly in your exams, it was either because you weren't bright enough or you were lazy. This turns out to be another of those pernicious over simplifications.

First, exams like GCSEs and A levels are competitive. Not everyone can be a 'winner'. There have to be a good number of 'losers' in order to make success worth having. If everyone got four As at A level they would be of no use to employers or admissions tutors, would they? Here's a thought experiment. It is the morning when everyone gets their A level results letter, and your daughter is waiting anxiously for the post. She opens it and finds that she has got her four As. She rings her best friend, Rachel, and is (mostly) pleased to find that Rachel has got four As too. They go down to the school and are surprised to discover that everyone in the school who sat A levels that year has got four As. And then, on the news that night, it is reported that every single candidate in the country achieved four As. Just imagine her emotional trajectory throughout the day, from delight, to pleasure (tinged with a bit of competitiveness), to puzzlement, to dejection and despair! In reality, examination boards (and politicians) are constantly tinkering with pass marks and grade boundaries to ensure that nothing like this fantasy can actually happen. A lot of children have got to do badly at the examination game; it's a statistical necessity. It's deceitful to claim that everyone can win if they try hard enough.

On the traditional view, intelligence is something that neither you nor your teachers could do anything about: it was largely decided by your genes. A lot of children come to believe, from pretty early on, that they are destined to be the losers – and it is because, in Jack Dee's words, you are just thick. But we know this isn't true. Children's performance at school depends on a host of other factors, such as whether they are worried about what is going on at home, whether they have a good teacher, whether they like their teacher, whether they are willing to devote their intelligence to things that seem pointless, whether their experience has taught them that trying hard is usually worthwhile, whether they much prefer practical and active learning to academic and sedentary learning, and so on. If your child is struggling at school, one thing is certain: it is *not* because they are stupid.

The importance of beliefs

One factor that makes a huge difference to how well children learn, in school and out, is what Stanford researcher Professor Carol Dweck has called a growth mindset.[8] Over decades of painstaking analysis of pupils, Dweck has been able to show that there are two broad categories of learners. One she calls 'fixed mindset' and the other 'growth mindset'. Some children have picked up the idea that their intelligence is basically limited to however much 'brains' they were born with. If they can't do something easily, they quickly conclude they just haven't got what it takes, and

---

8   There are many books you could read here, but perhaps the most accessible is Carol Dweck's *Mindset: The New Psychology of Success* (New York: Random House, 2006).

that's that. By contrast, there are other children who believe that their brains are more like muscles; they get stronger and smarter through exercise. So they like it when they have to think and try hard, because they see this as mental exercise and an opportunity to get smarter. They see their ability as expandable rather than predetermined. Here's the kicker: children who have growth mindsets consistently outperform their classmates on public examinations *and* are generally better at doing all the things that successful people tend to do (e.g. managing their emotions, coming up with creative ideas, having a go at new things). It is not just how clever you are (as measured by some kind of IQ test) that matters, but how you think about 'ability' itself. Those who believe that they can get smarter normally can, if they try. Which of these two groups would you want your child to be in?

Can you move someone from a fixed mindset to a growth mindset? And if so, how? The answers to these two questions are 'yes' and 'by helping them to think differently about the reasons for their successes and failures'. The best way to help someone develop a growth mindset is through the way he or she is given feedback after any activity. For example, if you write an essay and your teacher simply says to you, "Well done, Luke, you're good at English," or even, "That wasn't so good, Anna, I don't think you're cut out to be a writer," all they are hearing is some generalised praise (or criticism) that applies to them *as people*. Feedback like this is known as 'person praise'; that's to say it focuses on the individual rather than on what they have actually done to contribute to the grade achieved.

As a teacher or a parent it is easy to give this kind of feedback in the belief that we will be motivating the recipient. We'll be encouraging Luke if we keep telling him how gifted and talented he is. But we are not! We may even be damaging his likelihood of success. The most useful thing that parents and teachers can do is to give learners accurate, specific feedback on things they have done, especially noting where they have shown particular initiative or spent extra time on some aspect of an assignment. How you praise children really matters.[9] Growth mindset learners make more mistakes – and more *interesting* mistakes – than those with fixed mindsets. Why? Because we learn most when we are pushing ourselves, not merely staying within our comfort zone, but exerting ourselves to try something more challenging or adventurous.

It follows that schools which understand the power of a growth mindset will, paradoxically, see making mistakes (interesting, not just slipshod) as something to be encouraged. If you visit such schools, as we do, you will see some subtle differences. For example, in assemblies, as well as celebrating the successes of the First XI, groups of students who have gone the extra mile and really put in effort are routinely acknowledged. In classrooms it is common to have work in progress – warts and all – on display, as well as beautifully mounted examples of final 'products'. If you are a designer, engineer, musician or actor reading this you will perhaps recognise these as the prototypes or drafts which are essential to eventual success in the real world. The willingness to venture and tinker are as vital to real-world achievement as any innate talent or intelligence you might possess. And these attitudes of tinkering and trying are learned. Schools either strengthen or weaken them.

---

9 See Po Bronson, How not to talk to your kids: the inverse power of praise, *New York* magazine (3 August 2007). Available at: http://nymag.com/news/features/27840/.

We're creating a fear culture within education – if you don't achieve results *you have failed.* Teachers working in that fear culture narrow their curriculum to achieve that one objective. Leaders working in that fear culture hammer the creativity out of teachers if what they do doesn't lead to that one objective. And the people in charge then look for culprits in terms of school leaders who aren't doing what they want. I'm not the only head who's resigned; there are lots. This fear culture is preventing people from developing children and staff to full capacity. If you create fear in a culture, people will do what the people above them tell them to do – nothing else.

Neil, primary head teacher, Manchester

Some traditionalists are very strongly attached to the fixed mindset view. They are likely to think the previous paragraphs are so much 'wishy-washy liberal nonsense' and sneer at the research – because it is inconvenient for their world view. They like the idea that intelligence is fixed because it justifies a segregated education system, traditionally based on IQ. They will say that we need to sort out the sheep from the goats, those who have what it takes from those who don't. Schooling is expensive so, of course, there needs to be a separate stream for 'the brightest and the best' – thus defined – that runs from grammar and independent schools through to Oxford and Cambridge. But the static, fixed view of intelligence or 'ability' on which this reasoning rests is wrong. Children's *apparent* intelligence varies hugely from context to context, and depends on all kinds of factors

– like their *beliefs* about intelligence – which have nothing to do with any innate ability.[10]

The lure of Big Hard Data

To get to where schools need to go, we have to question the importance of standardised tests and the numbers they generate. Although they give the appearance of objectivity and reliability, these kinds of tests can hold back innovation if important things that cannot easily be quantified are discounted. One set of figures, produced by the Organisation for Economic Co-operation and Development (OECD) is especially influential at the moment. Let's have a look at them.

The OECD was set up in 1948 to run the Marshall Plan which was designed to rebuild a Europe ravaged by war. Today, more than 60 years later, it promotes policies to improve the economic and social well-being of people around the world. In terms of education, it is perhaps best known for its PISA (Programme for International Student Assessment) tests. Every three years it tests 15-year-olds across a range of subjects to see what they know and what they can do. (Remember the 'what they can do' part of this sentence because we will be returning to it, and it's very important.)

---

10 If you still need to be convinced, try reading David Perkins, *Outsmarting IQ: The Emerging Science of Learnable Intelligence* (New York: Free Press, 1995); Keith Stanovich, *What Intelligence Tests Miss: The Psychology of Rational Thought* (New Haven, CT: Yale University Press, 2009); or Robert Sternberg, *Beyond IQ: A Triarchic Theory of Human Intelligence* (Cambridge: Cambridge University Press, 1984). They are all very accessible.

Politicians across the world are scared of PISA results because they operate as a very public examination of every country's education ministry. Countries are ranked according to their performances. Here are the top three countries/cities in each test followed by the highest ranking European country followed by the UK's position using the 2012 results:

Maths

1.   Shanghai, China
2.   Singapore
3.   Hong Kong, China
9.   Switzerland
26. UK

Reading

1.   Shanghai, China
2.   Hong Kong, China
3.   Singapore
6.   Finland
23. UK

Science

1.   Shanghai, China
2.   Hong Kong, China
3.   Singapore
5.   Finland
20. UK[11]

Newspapers love these league tables too because it makes for easy journalism to print numerical rankings such as these. Journalists from countries whose students appear in the top 10 write pages of copy praising their country's education

---

11 See http://www.oecd.org/pisa/keyfindings/pisa-2012-results.htm.

system and schools. Those who feature much lower down the list like the UK (and the USA) scratch their heads and criticise teachers and schools and incumbent politicians. Employers use the PISA results as a chance to make statements about their country's respective global competitiveness. You can see why politicians are scared of PISA!

But what about parents? What do they think? Most of them are downright confused. How can the UK be so far down the list when we have so many world-class engineers, scientists, architects and writers? How is it that we have so many Nobel Prize winners in science and medicine? How come we have so many wonderful universities? At a local level, parents may draw comfort (or concern) from the performance of their own child's school which seems to be better/worse than the UK's showing in PISA. For many parents, high-stakes test results like these can contribute to a sense of unease about what their child's school is or is not teaching.

A few determined parents go online, look at the OECD's website and find out more about the tests. They quickly discover that the rankings are based on the results of two-hour paper and pencil tests. Some begin to wonder how reliable such tests can possibly be as a judgement on an individual's subject knowledge, let alone as an indicator of 'what they can do'. Those parents who keep searching quickly discover that the OECD is itself concerned about such limitations. To counter them it introduced a new creative problem-solving test in 2012 (the UK came eleventh in this new test). The creative problem-solving test is "an assessment of student performance in creative problem solving, which measures students' capacity to respond to non-routine situations in order to achieve their potential as constructive and reflective citizens."[12]

Sounds interesting, you may be thinking. But read on and you discover that this test is entirely computer-based. You are left with a slight niggle that, useful as computers are, screen-based performance may not always be a reliable indicator of real-world problem-solving.

But you've got the OECD bit between your teeth by now and you keep searching. Surely, you think, such an important organisation as the OECD must have done some more nuanced thinking about what it is that children need to learn today? You type 'OECD' and 'what children need to learn today' into your search engine and, lo and behold, you discover some discussions about the purpose and future of education (much more interesting than those simplistic league tables) which have left you wanting to know more. You happen upon a fascinating blog by Charles Fadel on an OECD site promoting discussion about what students should learn in the 21st century. His questions really make you think:

Should engineering become a standard part of the curriculum? Should trigonometry be replaced by more statistics? Is long division by hand necessary? What is significant and relevant in history? Should personal finance, journalism, robotics, and other new disciplines be taught to everyone – and starting in which grade? Should entrepreneurship be mandatory? Should ethics

---

12 See OECD, *PISA 2012 Results: Creative Problem Solving: Students' Skills in Tackling Real-Life Problems* (Volume V). Available at: http://www.oecd.org/pisa/keyfindings/pisa-2012-results-volume-v.htm.

be re-valued? What is the role of the arts – and can they be used to foster creativity in all disciplines?[13]

At the weekend, you find yourself having dinner with friends and conversation turns to the schools your friends' kids go to. As it happens – for the convenience of this imaginary example – one couple sends theirs to a private school, another to the local state one and a third to the latest example of a new kind of school in England. Let's call it a free school.

Questions breed more questions as the wine flows. How much history do you need to learn? Are you stupid if you can't recall the date of the Great Fire of London? Is Google dumbing us down? Is Google opening up a brave new world? Should all children be taught how to spot bias online? When do you need to know Newton's laws of motion? Do you need to know Newton's laws of motion at all? How is your daughter taught to do long multiplication or long division? Is it better or worse than the way you remember learning how to do it? And so on.

Later, you go back to your internet search and find out some more about the author of that OECD blog. Charles Fadel, it turns out, is also at Harvard, where he is thinking about how we can change the way we design the curriculum of schools. You light upon a helpful paragraph of his (which seems to be reflecting our experience with the Trads):

---

13 Charles Fadel, What should students learn in the 21st century?, *Education Today* (18 May 2012). Available at: http://oecdeducationtoday.blogspot. co.uk/2012/05/what-should-students-learn-in-21st.html.

Conversations about education abound with false dichotomies, and absolutist views, that must be transcended.

The lack of a balanced conversation leads to many OR debates; for instance:

- Knowledge OR skills.
- Science/Technology/Engineering/Math (STEM) OR Humanities/Arts.
- Didactic OR constructivist learning.
- Formal OR informal learning.
- All technology OR no technology.
- Character developed at school OR at home.

The balanced reality is that these are all AND propositions, working in concert with each other, and reinforcing each other, in a judicious, impactful feedback loop.[14]

These kinds of tensions, and the questions they generate, are exactly the kinds of issues we need to be grappling with. We'll be adding some more of our own to this list as we go through the book. But it isn't easy.

14 See http://www.thefivethings.org/charles-fadel/.

The Sabre-Tooth Curriculum

But before we go any further let's deal with a question that seems to us to be one of the most important of all:

Should we expect the curriculum to change significantly as the world out there changes, *or* are there some things that we just have to know and just have to be able to do whatever age we live in? (And is this really an *and*?)

And related to this:

To what extent should we teach things just in case they might be useful at some unknown time in the future, rather than at the time we *need* to know them in order to get something done that matters to us? (And is this an *and* too?)

Let's approach these questions via a story from the earliest beginnings of education. In 1939, an American scholar called J. Abner Peddiwell published an article about the earliest known form of education. He traced it back to the Chellean period, about half a million years ago, and specifically to an innovative individual called New-Fist-Hammer-Maker, or New-Fist for short. New-Fist thought children's play should be directed more purposefully towards the acquisition of useful skills. These included grabbing fish from the nearby pools, clubbing the little woolly horses that grazed on the edge of the forest for their meat and leather, and using firebrands to scare off the sabre-tooth tigers that came sniffing around at night. The village agreed, and so the first curriculum was born.

All went well with the Sabre-Tooth Curriculum until, gradually, over hundreds of years, the climate became wetter and colder. The ponds became cloudy so it was no longer possible to see the fish to grab them; they had to be caught using a net. The land became marshy, and the slow-footed woolly horses migrated east, to be replaced by much fleeter antelopes that could not be crept up on, but could only be shot with bows and arrows. Sabre-tooth tigers too moved away and instead came fierce grizzly bears that were not at all afraid of fire, but had to be trapped in camouflaged bear-pits dug on their trails.

One of New-Fist's descendants, Shoe-Stitcher, took stock of the situation and realised that the children's curriculum needed to change. Instead of grabbing fish with their bare hands, they should learn net-making. Instead of horse-clubbing, they needed to learn how to make bows and arrows and shoot straight. Instead of making flaming torches, children needed to learn how to dig the right size pits, and how to disguise them with branches and leaves. But the Board of Education strongly disagreed. The minutes of the critical meeting record the chairman as explaining that these new abilities were mere technical skills, whereas the traditional curriculum developed properly educated bodies and minds. In rather patronising language, he explains:

Don't you understand? We don't now teach fish-grabbing to grab fish; we teach it to develop a generalised agility which can never be developed by mere training. We don't teach horse-clubbing to club horses; we teach it to develop a generalised strength in the learner which he could never get from so prosaic and specialised a thing as antelope-shooting. We don't teach tiger-scaring simply to scare tigers. Oh dear me no. We teach it for the purpose of cultivating a noble courage which carries over into all the affairs of life, and which can never come from so base an activity as pit-digging.[15]

But Shoe-Stitcher was not to be shut up so easily. "Can't you see that times have changed?" he said in exasperation. "Why could we not develop those generalised qualities by teaching the children something really useful?" At this the chairman became even more pompous and hectoring:

If you had any education yourself, you would know that the essence of true education is timelessness. It is something that endures through changing conditions like a solid rock standing squarely and firmly in the middle of a raging torrent. You must know that there are some eternal verities – and the Sabre-Tooth Curriculum is one of them![16]

This modern fable was actually composed by a bona fide, though mischievous, academic professor by the name of Harold Benjamin. What do you think? Are there eternal verities which you would want your children to learn? Or are there things which your children are learning which

---

15 J. Abner Peddiwell (Harold Benjamin), *The Sabre-Tooth Curriculum* (New York: McGraw-Hill, 1939). We have adapted and abridged the original to save space.

16 Peddiwell, *The Sabre-Tooth Curriculum*.

seem to you to fall into the category of 'fish-grabbing'? If so, what are they?

It seems to us that the Trads are often unable to say why we should not be teaching net-making, archery and bear-pit-digging (or, in our case, computer-coding, internet-mental-health-protecting and public-figure-lie-detecting). We suspect that Mods, on the other hand, would find much enjoyment, as well as food for thought, in this parable. It will chime with their doubts about whether all children today really need to learn how to add fractions, solve quadratic equations and tell a sine from a tangent or a gerund from a gerundive. There will always be a minority of children who might go on to use these skills and knowledge in their professional lives, and a slightly larger minority who will simply enjoy mastering the rules of micro-worlds such as algebra and trigonometry. But there are millions of youngsters for whom these subjects are just a pointless grind, and there are a thousand other topics one could argue for with equal justification: Sudoku, crossword puzzles and *Minecraft*, to name just a few.

The belief that calculus, for example, is an essential part of the preparation for life for all young people is just that, a belief, not an established fact. There is no evidence that youngsters who are made to study trigonometry lead lives that are any more fulfilled or intelligent than those who are not. And there are lots of good free courses online (e.g. from the Khan Academy) that will get you quickly up to speed if and when you need it. (If you are not a teacher, when was the last time you needed, in your real life, to solve a quadratic equation? Or recall, without recourse to your iPad, the capital city of Mongolia? Or explain the difference between a terminal and a medial moraine, or a breve and a minim?)

The question of what is really worth knowing, in the Google age, is wide open, and one we will return to in Chapter 4.

School and real-world learning

If school is meant to offer young people a powerful preparation for a successful life (and not just for university), why isn't it more *like* real life? The way learning is organised in schools seems, in many respects, very different from, or even at odds with, the experience of learning that people have in their homes, workplaces, playgroups, sports and athletic clubs, online chatrooms and meditation retreats or when watching gardening or cookery programmes on television.

One of the classes that I teach are Year 11, the very bottom class, not doing GCSEs because it's thought that they're not capable of it. Instead they're doing a BTEC qualification in science. Teaching them essentially becomes an exercise in getting them copying stuff off the board, out of textbooks, off the internet. Absolutely no learning is going on at all. Their understanding is no greater than before. It is entirely an exercise in filling in loads of paperwork to get them a qualification. These are kids who are mostly very vulnerable, they have really complicated special educational needs. Pushing them through the system to get this totally irrelevant qualification, that's got nothing to do with their lives, is a complete waste of their time and a complete waste of my time. It's completely insane, and doesn't help anyone. There are so many more important things that we could be doing to prepare those kids for the world.

Kate, trainee science teacher, West London

Nearly 30 years ago, Professor Lauren Resnick, then president of the American Educational Research Association, gave a presidential address which was entitled, 'Learning in school and out'.[17] She pinpointed, on the basis of a wide variety of research, some key ways in which learning in school frequently differed from learning in these out-of-school situations. First, real-world learning is often collaborative whereas learning in school has traditionally been predominantly solo. Even where schools do lots of group-work, come exam time everyone has to revert to individual pieces of work for which they alone can be held responsible. Educationalists are beginning to devise ways of assessing collaborative endeavours, but they are in their infancy as yet.

Second, assessment in school is usually based on the ability to explain, describe, analyse or compute something. It is based on products that mostly involve manipulating symbols on paper or screen. In real-world learning the hallmark of success is usually practical: did the baby get to sleep? Did the bridge stay steady when people walked across it? Did the painting get accepted for the show? Do people come back to the restaurant? In a music exam or a driving test, you may have to do a bit of theory, but the acid test is visible in the way you actually do something. Real-world learning is about getting things done; in school it is about generating 'performances of understanding' for the sake of showing that you

17 Lauren Resnick, The 1987 presidential address: learning in school and out, *Educational Researcher* 16(9) (1987): 13–20.

can. People who are good at doing, but not very good at explaining, are massively handicapped in school by this difference.

Third, in the real world we learn because we want or need to – in order to achieve a goal that we ourselves consider worthwhile. Learning connects directly with the work or life situations in which we find ourselves. In school, by contrast, you are required to take on trust the idea that, someday, all this will make sense and turn out to be really useful – but not yet. And the timetable of what you are learning is dictated by someone else. The reason you are learning this now is because it is the next lesson in the teacher's scheme of work, not because you and your friends have stumbled on an interesting question that you feel motivated to pursue, or because your iPad suddenly won't connect to iTunes. So the motivation is quite different in school and out. And not all youngsters are willing or able to mobilise their full intelligence if they do not value what they are being asked to do. Many of them are mistakenly judged to be 'less intelligent' because of this.

Fourth, learning in the real world is very often accomplished with a whole array of tools and resources that are marshalled and drawn upon as necessary. In the real world we are mostly 'me plus': me plus my computer, me plus my iPhone, me plus all my notes and books, me plus all my contacts, me plus my mug of coffee. A plumber is completely hamstrung without her socket set and her mobile phone. When she meets an unfamiliar boiler and needs to call her contact in the parts department of the manufacturer, nobody would dream of calling that cheating. School traditionally tries to strip down learning so that it becomes the manipulation of words, numbers, chemical symbols or algebraic equations by a solitary mind.

Sugata Mitra, one of the most interesting and renowned educational thinkers in the world right now, has said that he could transform education with a single change: simply allow everyone to take their smartphone or their Wi-Fi-enabled tablet into the examination hall. Why create this artificial barrier? It's like taking Ronnie O'Sullivan's snooker cue away and saying, "Now show me how good you are." (There's more about Mitra in Chapters 4 and 7.)

Fifth, real-world learning is often physical. It involves the body in a variety of ways. Cooking, hairdressing, caring for young children or old people, wiring an electric circuit and playing netball all involve bodily activities such as bending, kneading, touching, listening and smelling, as well as taking care of your implements and materials. In school, subjects assume importance in inverse proportion to the amount of bodily activity they involve. If you can stay clean and still while you are learning, that is good, so maths and English come out at the top of the pecking order. Traditionalists can't wait to introduce students to the pristine abstract worlds of subjunctive clauses and Pythagoras' theorem. History and geography are a bit messier. Art and music are pulled down the hierarchy by their essentially sensory natures. Media and business studies are tainted by association with the real worlds of television and commerce.

And down the bottom of the pecking order come dance, drama, design technology and PE. Cookery, dressmaking, woodwork and metalwork are so shamefully reminiscent of old-fashioned trades and crafts that they cannot be spoken of directly; they now inhabit a shadow world of food technology and resistant materials. Instead of learning how to bake Mary Berry's amazing tiramisu cake, you study 'nutritional properties' and 'packaging and labelling', the curriculum being designed to drag students back from the ghastly brink of real physicality into the safe, clean – and, it has to said, often cheap – world of categories and issues. Youngsters who are best at thinking while they are doing tend to drift down this hierarchy of esteem, not because they are less able but because they find it difficult to master the peculiar trick of detaching cognition from action. It may be a worthwhile trick to master, but, because of the simplistic 'folk psychology' that underpins much of education, students are not *helped* to do so.

* * *

Why are schools designed in this dysfunctional way? Because when they were being developed in the 18th and 19th centuries, they were built on a false view of the human mind. They aimed to develop a general-purpose, all-round educated person by making school a place separate from life where there were no *specific* goals to which learning could become attached. This meant knowledge and skills would be represented in children's heads in a generic, free-floating way, waiting to be 'hooked' by any relevant need or circumstance that subsequently came along. School learning was made to be 'off the job', so to speak, so that what was learned would be retrievable under all appropriate circumstances.

But sadly the mind doesn't work like that. Every experience we have is indexed in the neural memory store in terms of the context in which, and the purpose for which, it was learned. What was going on? Where was I? How was I feeling? What was I up to? Did it work well? Everything we learn is automatically tagged in terms of these markers. We need these tags to tell us when to retrieve something we know and activate it. So there is no off the job; wherever we are, we are noticing our surroundings and our own priorities, and what we learn is registered and recorded in that context. School is definitely not off the job. It is not an absence of those cues and concerns; it is a very particular, and in many ways peculiar, constellation of cues and concerns. The miracle is that some of what we learn in school *does* stay with us and comes to mind when it is needed in the outside world. Sadly a huge amount of school learning does not.

This doesn't mean that we can't help learning to become gradually more generic or disembedded. We can. The point is that the broader relevance and utility of what you are learning has to be discovered. Transfer is also a learning job, and it is one often neglected by traditional teachers, carrying a naive theory of mind, who vaguely assume that if you have learned something 'properly', if you were 'paying attention', then transfer ought, magically, to happen. It doesn't. If you want your students to develop those more general-purpose learning skills and attitudes you have to work at it by, for example, varying the contexts and the tasks, and explicitly getting them to discover for themselves which of the habits and procedures they are developing apply when.

If your child is struggling at school it may well be because of the peculiar nature of school itself, not because they are 'low ability' or 'unmotivated'. These labels simply conceal all the deeper questions that need to be addressed. We hope that this discussion might help you to shift the conversations you are having with teachers on to a more productive plane.

When I was in Year 8, I sat next to a very quiet student in my English class. One day I caught sight of her cutting her wrists with the point of her compass. It was in plain view during our lesson …

Several people missed terms at a time for feeling depressed, and some were admitted at eating disorder clinics. I myself had an eating disorder between 13 and 17. Norms are powerful at school, and it just so happened that one of the norms at my school was to have a thigh the same size as your calf. I never told my school, and my school never suspected anything – it was the norm so I was no anomaly. I think I felt out of control and anxious about being valued. Maybe this was a symptom of the systematic disempowerment of young people at school, although there were definitely other factors aside from school.

The academic pressure is ridiculous. I was once told by my statistics teacher that I was spreading myself 'too thin' and that if I wanted to carry on with maths the next year, I needed to stop doing so many extra-curricular activities. This was despite me scoring 94% average. People have totally lost sight of what learning is about in the first place!

**Natasha, undergraduate, previously at an
independent secondary school**

Chapter 3

Competence and character

Intelligence plus character – that is the goal of true education.

Martin Luther King

We'd like you to try another thought experiment. It's in two parts. In the first part you will finally meet the Ruby who gave this book its title. Imagine you are the head of a secondary school and you are walking down the street when you are stopped by an ex-student who left about two years ago. Ruby says she just wants to thank you for the great education she got at your school. You remember Ruby well, so you recall that she left at 16 with two rather poor GCSEs (a D in drama and an E in English). So you scratch around for a response. (You can tell she is being sincere.) You say, "Ah yes, I remember you had a big part in the really successful performance of *The Crucible*, didn't you? And I know you made some great friendships." "True," says Ruby, "but that's not what I'm talking about. I'm talking about the quality of the *education* you gave me. It was wonderful. Really." And now you are rather flummoxed, and you say, "Sorry, Ruby, I don't understand what you mean."

The question is: what does Ruby say? How can Ruby honestly feel that those years were well spent, when she was a 'loser' at the examination game? You might like to discuss this with someone before you read on. (You might like to be reading this book with someone else – your partner, your child, your mother – so you can discuss and argue along the way.)

Here is the kind of thing that we think Ruby might say. We've neatened up her words so this is partly our voice, as well as Ruby's. But see if you think this is plausible.

You helped me develop my *self-confidence*. By that I mean you treated me in ways that helped me build my self-respect. You taught me that, even though I wasn't an egg-head, I wasn't stupid. By the way your teachers responded to me, you gave me faith that what I thought was worth thinking. You helped me to become optimistic and positive in my outlook on life. You gave me the feeling that there were many worthwhile things I could achieve and become, if I put my mind to it, even though they were not academic things. All of the teachers in your school believed in us, and so helped us to believe in ourselves. And you made me discover that, if I put in the effort, it often paid off. By pushing me and not giving up on me, you helped me learn to be a can-do sort of person.

You helped me become *curious*. When I asked questions your teachers didn't make me feel stupid or tell me 'I should have been listening'. If my questions were a bit wacky you explained why in a respectful way. You made me feel that the questions I asked were worth asking, even though there wasn't always time in class to go into them. You encouraged us all to try new things, and made it so nobody ever laughed at anyone for having a go, even if they weren't very good to start with. I learned that everyone makes mistakes: it doesn't mean you are no good, it means you are learning. So I'm always up for a challenge now, and I'm exploring all kinds of things I would never have dreamed of – especially through books. You really helped me to see reading as a pleasure, not a drudgery. And you encouraged us to question what we were being told (or what we read, especially on the net). We could always say, "Hang on a minute, Miss, how do we know that's true?" And your teachers would say, "Fair point, Ruby – how could we check?" So now I'm quite bold about challenging things I read or am being told (but in the respectful way you modelled for us).

You helped us all become *collaborative* kinds of people. Sometimes you called it 'conviviality', and talked of the friendship and comradeship that learning so often requires. Your teachers showed us how to discuss and disagree respectfully, so we naturally treated each other like that. I'm now not afraid to ask for help, or to offer it when I think someone needs it. You taught us never to laugh at anyone just because they didn't know something. I learned to be more open and friendly to new people and to want to help them fit in and feel at home. We were a very non-cliquey school. I learned to be a good team player, and to know when to button my lip (that took some learning, but it was worth it). I think I'm more generous-spirited than I was. And I'm definitely a better friend: you helped us understand why it is so important, for our own sake, to be trustworthy and honest in our dealings with people – and to admit when we had screwed up or apologise when we said something out of order.

You definitely helped me become a better *communicator*. Because I learned to enjoy reading, I think I have a better understanding of people and a richer vocabulary – especially for talking about emotional or intimate kinds of things. I like looking up new words and trying them out. I love how we can be really into what Liam called 'the craic' one minute, just joshing and having fun, and then we can switch to being serious and soft if someone is troubled about something. We talked a lot in class, and your teachers helped us to recognise the different kinds of talk we could have, and how to be appropriate. And I learned that sometimes I need to be quiet and by myself too, and that doesn't mean I'm shy or upset. I've learned that sometimes I need to stop and think before I speak – but not always. And I'm happy to talk to anyone – teachers, strangers, my friends' grandparents ... even the Queen if she came by! It's part of being confident, I suppose, and not being on edge that what I say might be stupid.

You helped me discover my own *creativity*. Your teachers often set us puzzles and asked us for our ideas, so we got used to thinking aloud and building on what other people had said. We learned not to dismiss things that sounded daft too quickly, because they could often lead to interesting and novel ideas. Your teachers often set us great projects that really stretched us to achieve more than we thought we could. And there were plenty of opportunities (though not always in lessons) for us to pursue our own interests and experiments, and to learn to think for ourselves and come up with our own proposals. You gave us opportunities to be funny and zany, and you also made us think about our own education and come up with suggestions for improvement that you took seriously. Some teachers even taught us how to do wacky things like learn to toggle between being clear and logical and then going dreamy and imaginative – how to control our own minds better to get the most out of them.

You helped us all discover the value of being *committed* to what we do. Through being given the chance to learn independently, you helped me learn to take responsibility, to sort things out for myself and to stick with hard things and not wait to be rescued. (I remember one assembly where you talked about Ricky Gervais discovering what he called 'the joy of the struggle': I've never forgotten that.) Teachers used to go on a bit about 'resilience', but I think I have really learned how to be patient and persistent, and to know when to push myself and when it is smart to take a break and cool off. I'm not afraid of hard work, and you showed me that worthwhile things usually don't come easily, so when I do go to university (I will, you know) I will be ready for the self-discipline and slog I will need to put in.

And you also taught me the pleasures of *craftsmanship*. I used to be a bit slapdash, but now I take a real pride in producing work that is as good as I can make it. I mean college work – homework assignments and so on – but also when I practise the guitar the week before we have band rehearsal. I don't want to let the others down, but, more importantly, I don't want to let myself down. It's not just about determination; it's about being careful, and thinking about what you are doing, and taking time to reflect and improve, and going over your mistakes and practising the hard parts. You used to talk to us about the three Es of 'good work' – being engaging, being excellent and being ethical (I think it was from some prof at Harvard). I liked the ethical bit. My friends laugh, but when we are writing lyrics I won't stand for anything sexist or abusive these days! I want what I do to be, not goody-goody, but good in all three ways.

Now, obviously we have made Ruby up, but we think what she says is really important. She is trying to capture another side to what goes on in schools which, when it works well, produces more young people who are enterprising, friendly, moral and imaginative. She has tried to capture them in what we call the seven Cs: confidence, curiosity, collaboration, communication, creativity, commitment and craftsmanship. This, in a nutshell, is the 'other game' of school. If you cannot be a winner at the grade game, you can still come away having been a winner at the character game. The first requires losers; anyone can win the second. And the second actually counts for more in the long term, in real life.

If you had longer, Ruby could have told you about her friend, Nadezna, who was not so fortunate. She went to a school down the road where instead of the seven Cs she learned the seven Ds. Instead of becoming confident she became defeated. Instead of developing curiosity Nadezna became disengaged. Instead of collaboration she developed distance from all but members of her own gang – her world became split into a very narrow group of *us* and a very large group consisting of everyone else called *them*. Instead of communicative she became, with the wider world, largely dumb (or at least monosyllabic). Instead of becoming creative she became deadbeat: passive and lethargic. Instead of committed she has become a drifter, unable to stick at anything, moving on whenever things threaten to get difficult. And instead of cultivating craftsmanship she has become a dogsbody, capable only of menial tasks and unable to raise her game when greater precision or responsibility is required. Between Ruby and Nadezna there is, of course, a whole spectrum of attitudes – but we know which end we want our children, grandchildren, nieces and nephews to head towards.

* * *

One of the absurdities of the current education system is the single-minded obsession with results at any price – especially at secondary school. Schools are judged on the examination performance – mainly at GCSE and A level – they manage to wring out of children, regardless of whether this is appropriate or of any collateral damage that may be caused. We'll come back to this later, but just a quick illustration here will do. In England, there is a very important metric by which schools are judged. It is the percentage of students who manage to attain a C grade or better in at least five subjects, of which two must be English and maths (soon to be superseded by the even more stringent Progress 8).[1] If your 15-year-old son is heading for a D in one of his GCSE subjects, but the school thinks that, with a bit of help he might just make a C, in many schools he will get extra tuition and a lot of coaxing and coaching. Transforming a D into a C counts for a lot, whereas transforming an E into a D doesn't. If he is not judged to be capable of getting a C, he won't get that attention. The quality of his teaching will vary dramatically, depending not on what suits him, nor on trying to get the best out of all pupils, but because schools need to game the system – and your son becomes a pawn in that game.

We were reminded of this when thinking about Ruby and Nadezna. How lovely it would be to be able to transform all of Nadezna's Ds into Ruby's Cs – for all the tens of thousands of Nadeznas there are out there. But that would be a very different ambition from the petty, pernicious little game that is played every year at the moment.

We don't think Ruby is at all unrealistic. We know schools, as you probably do, where a lot of care goes into creating a culture that successfully incubates qualities like the seven Cs; and we know schools that don't. And we don't think this is a reversion to some feeble and discredited notion of 'child-centred' or 'progressive' education. Our guess is that millions of parents would like their children to go to schools where values like these – some of them quite 'old fashioned', some more specialised for the modern world – are being explicitly cultivated; and millions of teachers who are not lucky enough to be working in such schools already would love to.

---

1 Progress 8 is the latest term for EBacc (a short form of English Baccalaureate), a deliberate attempt by government to control the subjects by which a school's success is measured.

- Are the seven Cs the kinds of attitudes you would like your children (or students) to have?

- Are the seven Cs ones that you think will help them to thrive in the 21st century?

- If you had to rank order the seven Cs, which would be at the top of your list? Which at the bottom? How would you adjust them?

- Do you think it is realistic to think about cultivating them explicitly (or is that pie in the sky)?

- If a school did pay more attention to this 'other game', do you think its results would go up or down?

- Are the seven Cs just for the 'low achievers' like Ruby, or are they appropriate – vital even – for the high fliers as well?

Talk amongst yourselves!

Now here's the second part of our thought experiment. It involves you being the head teacher again, but this time you are wandering down the High Street in Cambridge. As you are passing the offices of the University Counselling Service, the door opens and out in front of you steps Eric – who was one of your brightest students in the same year as Ruby, and left to read natural sciences at Trinity Hall. You are both a little embarrassed, but after a few stilted attempts at conversation you say you can't help but notice that he has been in the counselling offices, and you hope everything is all right. It patently isn't: Eric, who was a confident young man at your school, is now pale, withdrawn and having great difficulty making eye contact. You are finding it hard to hear what he is saying, but he mumbles something that sounds like "Feeling like a fraud". Overcome with concern for the dramatic change in Eric, you suggest a cup of tea which he warily accepts. What do you think is the story that he gradually reveals over tea? Do you find Eric plausible?

It turns out that Eric is all too real. A significant number of apparently bright, self-confident, articulate, high-achieving students will seek counselling during their under-graduate years at Oxford and Cambridge: that's several thousand young people.[2] There will be a variety of causes, obviously, but one of the major ones is this feeling that Eric is suffering from of having been found out, unmasked as an imposter – someone who, the evidence seems to suggest, is unworthy of being where they are. And that evidence is that they are now struggling with the weight and the difficulty of the work they are being set, yet they are supposed to be 'bright', and bright students are not supposed to struggle. Therefore, so the thought pattern goes, I must be more stu-pid than I and others believed, and so I am a fraud. This is a shattering realisation, so it is no surprise that anxiety and/or depression ensue.

So-called 'imposter syndrome' is on the rise, according to the directors of both the Oxford and Cambridge counsel-ling services, and one of the reasons is that schools are getting better at force-feeding and shoehorning their stu-dents through the syllabus, so they get the grades they need, but do so in a way that fails to prepare them for the demands of life after school. More modularising, more coaching, more detailed feedback from caring teachers about what exactly you need to improve if you are going to get the cov-eted A* in your A levels. All of this helps to get the grades, but systematically deprives students of opportunities – as

2 Warwick Mansell, 'Spoonfed' students lack confidence at Oxbridge, *TES* (10 December 2010). Available at: https://www.tes.co.uk/article. aspx?storycode=6065624.

one tutor put it to us – to learn how to 'flounder intelli-gently'. As we saw earlier, this is vital not only to cope when you are at university, but also to field that curve-ball question which you are sure to be tossed at interview. (We've used Cambridge as our example here, but we know that there are Erics in many universities and colleges.)

The same applies, by the way, in today's job market. Working for Google is a plum job, and they get thousands of applications. But, again, watch out for the questions they will ask your daughter at interview. If she is asked whether she has an IQ of over 130, warn her that there are right and wrong answers. Yes is the wrong answer. At Google, they think if you have bothered to take an IQ test, and have both-ered to remember the result, you may well be the kind of nerd who treasures badges of past accomplishments, rather than the kind of 'intelligent flounderer' they are looking for. At Google, intelligence does not mean being able to solve abstract logical puzzles under pressure. It means being able to think and question and learn in the face of unprece-dented problems for which there are as yet no right answers. Likewise, if they ask your daughter whether she has a track record of success, it is much better for her to say it is patchy than to edit her CV and pretend she is Little Ms Perfect. Crowing about the past doesn't cut it at Google; grappling with the future does. And some schools teach that, and many don't.

Education is not the same as school

To help get a handle on your worries about school, it might be useful to remember the difference between education and schooling. Education is a vision of what it is that our children will need if they are going to flourish in the world as we predict it will be: that is to say, in their world, not ours. What knowledge and skills, what attitudes and values will stand them in good stead as they embark on life in a globalised and digitised future? To decide on the core aims of education, therefore, we need imagination and philosophy. We need to imagine, as well as we can, what their world will be like – at a fairly broad level of generality. Education has to be meaningful and relevant to the software designers, hairdressers, financial advisers, plumbers, nurses, neurosurgeons and farmers of the future. So we have to think: what will be the demands, risks and opportunities of the world that we foresee? And what are the personal resources that will enable young people to cope with those demands, capitalise on those opportunities and live good lives as a result?

If the world they will experience is likely to make complex demands on their ability to be an honest and trustworthy friend, for example, what attitudes towards online relationships do we need to help them develop? If their world is likely to be full of options and uncertainties, how do we help them get ready to deal well with uncertainty and make careful and wholesome choices? If their world is going to contain a rapidly increasing number of old people (that's us), should education be aimed at producing young people who will naturally feel kind, caring, patient and responsible towards the elderly? That's the conversation of education. It is to do with what's left at the end of their formal educational experiences, the residues of that experience which will enable them to engage intelligently with the ups and downs that come their way. This is a moral conversation, and it is necessary and unavoidable. If people disagree about the aims of education, this has to be within a conversation about differing values and differing images of the future.

School, on the other hand, is a particular system that societies have invented for 'doing education'. Education is the ends; school is the means. The only way of deciding if a school is 'outstanding' or not is to refer back to our list of those desirable residues (the seven Cs), and judge it by its success at producing young people who fit the bill. Are we turning out a lot of Rubies and not many Erics? Are they helpful to old ladies in the supermarket who can't find the right money? Are they flourishing at university when the workload is a lot higher and the social safety net much weaker than they experienced at school? Are they able to have fun without becoming obnoxious or damaging their health (whether that be the arrogant posh boys of the Bullingdon Club trashing a country restaurant or local kids throwing up in a city centre on a Saturday night)?

Exams are a proxy for those desired residues, and we should be asking whether they are capturing, as well as they can, the qualities of character and mind we think our children will need. Is a medical student's performance in their examinations a good predictor of their clinical judgement or their bedside manner? (It isn't.) Does a theology student's level of moral reasoning, as measured on a test, correlate well with their actual honesty or kindness? (It doesn't.) A motor mechanic may have passed her apprenticeship exams, but if her welds break up when your car goes over a pothole then we need to find a new test. The test of schooling is not whether you can do well *at school* – or even whether you enjoyed your schooldays – but whether what you have done has prepared you effectively for something else: college, a job or life at large. Exams ought to do a reasonable job of predicting how someone actually functions in some context in the future. If they don't, they just become self-referring and self-serving. If people disagree about schooling, rather than about education, then this is a technical matter. Empirically, are schools delivering the benefits they claim to? And are the instruments they use to assess how well they are working appropriate?

The really important point to stress is that schools must always be trying to enhance young people's capabilities in some way. Which particular capabilities they are aiming at is a question of values; but at root, schools must be aiming to help people *do* something better out of school or after schooling has finished. Knowledge that gives you no practical purchase on the physical and social worlds beyond school is pointless. For example, if university entrance depended on your ability to recite screeds of nonsensical poetry – stuff that you mugged up just for a three-hour memory test, and then was generally agreed to have no further use or interest at all – there would surely be an outcry about wasting children's time and insulting their intelligence, and rightly so.

What do children really need to learn?

What Ruby and Eric teach us is that there is always a deeper agenda going on at school, which is about the cultivation of competence and character. It is what we called earlier the 'other game'. On the surface, school may seem to be all about the content – *learning about* things like the chemical elements or the Tudors – and the grades. But, implicitly or explicitly, you are also *learning to* do things: to respond in certain ways when particular things show up. At primary school you learned to hang up your coat, wait your turn, clear up after yourself and 'play nicely'. Gradually, as you move up, you learn to create a PowerPoint presentation, structure an essay, solve disputes and read your teacher's mind. Ruby has learned to hold her head up, to value her own curiosity, to get on well with people of all kinds, to pay careful attention to what she is doing, to manage her time and think for herself. Nadezna and Eric have learned different habits. Nadezna has learned to be slapdash; she doesn't know how to take pains over something or why she should. Eric has learned to respond to pressure by waiting to be rescued and reassured – and when he finds himself in a situation where that is not happening, he goes to pieces.

School should provide children with knowledge about the major problems that the world is facing. But we never really got proper education about climate change and biodiversity loss and the energy crisis and the financial crisis, and all of these things that are affecting children as they become modern citizens and workers in the world. How can we possibly be the generation who tries to solve these problems if we're not taught about them from an early age? I think that's a really big problem that school should address ... Instead, the school assumed that we all wanted to go to university, and that Oxbridge was right for everyone. They aren't thinking about your true desires and embracing the uncertainty of life. They didn't cater for us as individuals.

69

What school *didn't* equip me with was diversity – diversity of outlook, lifestyles, career choices. You need to be open-minded and flexible; you need to be willing to make yourself vulnerable, to really be able to connect with people, to really love them. For me school was: "You *will* do A levels, you *will* go to university, you *will* become a good citizen, you *will* have babies. The end." School is such a closed little environment. I didn't mentally mature until I left school. Even though I only left school last year, I feel I've learned so much about myself and my place in society. I've become a much more open-minded person in general. But I'm still worried that I won't take enough risks, that I won't go for things if the outcome is uncertain, that I won't travel places. It's easier to just slip into a comfortable job and group of friends. I don't want to do that.

Elsa, recently left an independent girls' school

At least as important as the accumulation of knowledge and understanding is the development of a range of useful real-world competences. A good part of education ought to be, we think, focused on making sure that young people can do a whole lot of things that they will very likely find useful. But what are the core competences for living safely, sociably and satisfyingly? Obviously, it will depend on the culture and circumstances into which you were born. But, broadly, can we pick out some general 'competences for living'? Here are some candidates. They were generated in the context of a very exciting 'global summit on education' held at the Perimeter Institute, an elite physics lab in Waterloo, Canada, in October 2013.[3] For five days, a group of around 30 young people from all around the world explored, with the help of some 'experts' (of which Guy was one) what the school of 2030 ought to look like. Here is one of the lists they came up with on 21st century competences:

- Self-protection – how to look after yourself, e.g. in strange or threatening situations.

- Inter-cultural – how to get along with folks different from yourself, e.g. empathy, tolerance.

- Finance – e.g. how to manage money, budgeting, protesting effectively about financial scandals.

- Sex – e.g. how to communicate verbally and non-verbally about needs, preferences and uncertainties, and about contraception; how to be sensual and sexual and sometimes wild.

- Manual/practical – e.g. how to use basic hand and power tools safely and appropriately.

- Science – how to engage with scientific discoveries, controversies and abuses, e.g. fracking, stem cell research; how to tell valid from bogus scientific claims – assessing evidence.

- Statistics – how to weigh up probabilities and operate intelligently in probabilistic situations, e.g. the risks of different medical treatments.

---

3   For more information, see Michael Brooks and Bob Holmes, *Equinox Blueprint: Learning 2030*. A Report on the Outcomes of the Equinox Summit: Learning 2030 convened by the Waterloo Global Science Initiative, Waterloo, Ontario, Canada, September 29 to October 3, 2013. Available at: http://www.wgsi.org/sites/wgsi-live.pi.local/files/Learning%202030%20Equinox%20Blueprint.pdf.

- Scepticism – how to spot sophistry and sloppy thinking in all areas of life.

- Talking – e.g. how to explain yourself clearly and confidently in all kinds of situations.

- Writing – how to write effectively in a variety of different 'voices', e.g. a business-like email, a love letter, a request for permission, a good story, a reflective journal.

- Reading – how to read in different ways and at different rates for different practical purposes and (very importantly) for pleasure.

- Navigation – how to orient yourself in space by using wind, compass, maps, geo-positioning gizmos, etc.

- Cookery – how to plan and make a nice meal from scratch.

- Horticulture – how to grow plants and plan a garden.

- Care – how to take care of creatures of all kinds and sizes, especially animals, babies and the elderly.

- Religion – how to find a non-exploitative setting for exploring deep questions and expressing honest experience.

- Relationships – how to behave graciously in company; how to help make collective decisions.

- Morality – how to behave well with other people, e.g. showing honesty, trustworthiness, integrity, moral courage, appreciation, generosity, forgiveness.

- Self-presentation – how to dress and groom yourself to achieve different purposes (e.g. an interview, a date) and for satisfying self-expression; clothes, hairstyle, jewellery, piercings, tattoos, etc.

● Driving – how to drive and look after a bicycle, a car, a motorbike, etc.

● Leisure – how to amuse yourself and find humour in situations without upsetting others.

● Fitness – how to choose and pursue forms of exercise that are fun and keep you fit.

● Relaxation – how to unwind after stress and release tension; positive kinds of 'self-soothing' and 'self-talk'.

● Attention – how to stay focused and concentrated when needs be, and how to detect useful, often subtle, cues in your world such as other people's non-verbal signals.

● Craftsmanship – how to be careful and accurate when needs be; how to produce your 'best work'.

As you read it, you might like to be mulling over these questions:

● Which of these do you think all youngsters ought to develop?

● Which do you think would happen without any special training or attention?

● Which are appropriate at what ages?

● Which do you think are appropriate/inappropriate matters for school?

● Which others would you want to add? Delete?

You'll immediately see there is a lot of ground for disagreement. But do you agree that this kind of competence has to be the starting point for thinking about what our children really need to be taught in the future? The group of young adults who thought up this list certainly thought so.

Habits of mind

This list of competences is a bit of a rag-bag. We could tidy it up somewhat by dividing it into two groups: what we might call *skills* – which are techniques that can be learned or trained quite explicitly – and what we will call *habits of mind* – which are more general tendencies to respond to events in a particular way. Solving simultaneous equations or making meringue is a skill. Handing in lost property or owning up when you have broken something are examples of a more general habit of mind called 'honesty'. Many people are drawing attention to the importance of these more general habits of mind these days. If children are to grow up with the ability to thrive in a challenging and fast-changing world, they say, it is things like Ruby's seven Cs that they are going to need. Two recent books provide comprehensive reviews of the research that shows how important these habits of mind are for success in life. They are *How Children Succeed: Grit, Curiosity and the Hidden Power of Character* by Paul Tough, and *Ungifted: Intelligence Redefined* by Scott Barry Kaufman.[4] Ruby, with her resources of commitment and confidence – a feeling of being able to direct her own life, and to put in the disciplined effort to achieve her goals – will do better in life, in every way you can think of, than Nadezna.

---

4 Paul Tough, *How Children Succeed: Grit, Curiosity and the Hidden Power of Character* (London: Random House, 2013); Scott Barry Kaufman, *Ungifted: Intelligence Redefined* (New York: Basic Books, 2013).

And the seven Cs should be on every school curriculum, because the research shows that these habits or qualities of mind can be developed quite deliberately. Optimism and commitment are not personality traits that are genetically locked in; they are habits that can be powerfully influenced by experience – at home, with friends and in school. (From an early age, friends and playmates have a surprisingly strong effect on the development of these lasting dispositions.) A great Russian psychologist, Lev Vygotsky, discovered long ago that (to paraphrase a little) minds are contagious: we pick up mental habits and attitudes from the people we hang out with. Minds rub off on each other, especially when we are young.

A salutary lesson was learned from the early wave of enthusiasm for what are called 'charter schools' in the United States. They were new schools that were, admirably, dedicated to 'getting poor kids to college', by hook or by crook. And with intensive support, dedicated coaching and high expectations many more of these students enrolled in college than would have been expected. So far so good. The problem was that most of them then dropped out. When they went on to college that high-powered support team was left behind, and without it many of those young people didn't know how to cope. They had got the grades, but they hadn't developed the resilience, independence and self-discipline that they now really needed.[5]

Paul Tough argues that it is especially youngsters from difficult backgrounds who need these qualities, because their social environments often don't provide the guidance and structure that is needed. If your family and friends aren't

---

5   For a critique of charter schools, you could try Naomi Klein, *The Shock Doctrine: The Rise of Disaster Capitalism* (London: Penguin, 2008).

supporting you in your studies, it is all the more important that you have developed those habits for yourself. And the charter schools left that bit out. But the existence of so many Erics shows us that more fortunate youngsters also need these attributes. When Eric went to Cambridge, he felt the loss of that caring, correcting support network as keenly as anyone, and was at sea without it. So the effort to build these mental and emotional habits is relevant, even essential, not just for poor kids; it is necessary for all our children. To cope well with tricky times you need more than a bag of knowledge and a clutch of certificates; you need a strong and supple mind.

The overwhelming conclusion of all this research is that grades are not enough. Getting the grades opens doors and broadens choice, and that's surely what any parent or teacher would want for their children. But, if they are to prosper once they have passed though those doors and made those choices, children also need these qualities and habits of mind. And it is open to any teacher to pay more attention to their cultivation. Bluntly, you can teach the Tudors in a way that develops the habits of independence, imagination, empathy and debate; or you can teach them in a way that develops passivity, compliance, credulity and memorisation. You can teach the water cycle in a way that stretches students' ability to dig deep in their learning and ask good questions; or you can teach it in a way that makes them dependent on their teacher and frightened of making mistakes. Both can get good results. Only one reliably develops the habits of mind they are going to need; the other increases the risk of becoming a Nadezna or an Eric.

Cultivating character

There are broadly three clusters of these character strengths that are (a) predictive of success in life and (b) capable of being cultivated by schools. The first is called rather grandly 'self-regulation'. It is the cluster of habits that enable you to concentrate despite distractions; to stay engaged despite being frustrated; to make short-term sacrifices in the interest of longer term gains; and to deal with frustration or disappointment. ('Self-soothing' is the fancy word for this last capacity.) These are the abilities that underpin self-control, self-discipline, emotional intelligence and will-power. Ruby called it 'commitment'. A massive study in New Zealand showed, beyond doubt, that the lack of these damages your life chances very significantly – whatever your grades.[6]

Self-discipline is very different from obedience. When children are disciplined they learn to do what others tell them – and not pursue goals and projects that *they* want to do. Obedient children learn to behave well to gain praise or rewards, and to avoid harsh words or punishment. Sometimes that may be necessary but it doesn't, of itself, develop those self-regulatory abilities. With self-regulation, children discover how to make life go more smoothly and satisfyingly for themselves. And it turns out that social games – whether it be creating an imaginative fantasy world, where everyone has their own 'character', or playing football in the yard – are powerful incubators of self-regulation. Put simply, you find out that it just doesn't work if you suddenly decide that you want to 'be the doctor' or to take your cricket bat home

---

6   See Terrie Moffitt, Louise Arseneault, Daniel Belsky, et al., A gradient of childhood self-control predicts health, wealth, and public safety, *Proceedings of the National Academy of Sciences of the USA* 108(7) (2011): 2693–2698.

if you are out for a duck. People get cross with you. You don't get invited to play next time. A way of teaching pre-schoolers in the United States called Tools of the Mind structures this kind of play – and it has shown that children develop self-regulation faster, and also show better development of literacy and numeracy. Self-regulation lays the foundations of being a more effective learner: less prone to frustration or distraction.[7]

The other two clusters are, if you like, the two main branches that grow out of this trunk of self-control. The first branch grows into the habits and attitudes of a 'good person': kind, friendly, generous, tolerant, empathic, forgiving, trustworthy, honest, having moral courage and integrity, and so on. Jihadist and racist groups would probably have a different list, but both humanism and the world's major religions agree on something like this. Most schools have some kind of moral code of this kind, though it is sometimes honoured more in rhetoric than reality. Traditionally, the 'learning methods' for developing these attitudes tended to focus more on the punishment of breaches than on the cultivation of strengths which, for the reasons just cited, tends to be less effective.

The second branch grows into the habits of mind that characterise a 'good learner'. While the virtues of a 'good person' seem relatively stable across time and culture, those of the 'good learner' are less familiar. Many take it for granted, however, that they are of real, practical relevance to young people embarking on life in a time of particular change, opportunity and uncertainty. The internet makes knowledge instantly available, and while Wikipedia is

7   See Paul Tough, Can the right kinds of play teach self-control?, *New York Times* (27 September 2009). Available at: http://www.nytimes. com/2009/09/27/magazine/27tools-t.html?pagewanted=all&_r=0 .

astonishingly accurate, it is also fallible. Young people need to be 'knowledge critics' and not just 'knowledge consumers'. In cyber-world, people are often not who they say they are, so young people, if they are to be safe, need to be 'identity critics' too. Learning is often hard, protracted and perplexing, so they need to be ready, willing and able to struggle and persist. Learning is often a collaborative rather than (or as well as) a solitary venture, so the inclination to be a good sounding board for others, and the ability to give feedback in a respectful and useful way and take criticism yourself without getting hurt and defensive, is also needed.

These learning attributes go by different names: 21st century skills, wider skills for learning, soft skills, non-cognitive skills, dispositions, character strengths or traits, attitudes and values. As we have explained, we think it's better not to use the word 'skills', but many people still do. And we could argue with some of these descriptions. Calling them 'soft' undervalues them and encourages people who don't immediately understand them to use such pejorative labels as 'touchy-feely', as if 'persisting in the face of difficulty' or 'looking at things through someone else's eyes' were too embarrassingly Californian to be taken really seriously by hard-headed grown-ups. 'Non-cognitive' isn't right either because that seems to imply 'emotional', and feeds into the mistaken view that emotions are somehow subversive of rigorous thinking. Concentration and imagination are highly 'cognitive' – if by that you mean 'essential to effective and creative problem-solving'.

In 2009, we were commissioned by the National Endowment for Science, Technology and the Arts (NESTA) to do a review of these different frameworks.[8] We found instances of these 'character specifications' from the national governments of, for example, Singapore, Australia, New Zealand, Finland and Ireland. Interestingly, several of these countries are at the top of the PISA tables, but they have become dissatisfied with a form of education that merely turns out, as some of them put it, 'test-passing robots'. They know that success in the modern world depends on attributes of mind and heart that are deeper than the ability to get your sums right. And they are desperately keen to know how these traits can be cultivated more systematically and more successfully in schools.

In brief

The best schools have always concerned themselves with the development of 'character'. Traditionally this meant being honourable, erudite and a 'good sport'. But today we need to think again: not about whether this concern is relevant – of course it is – but about exactly what characteristics are relevant for all in a socially, geographically, politically, digitally and cognitively complicated world.

Is this some kind of wishy-washy liberal agenda, designed to dumb down our youth by letting them run around like little savages and be completely self-indulgent, and fail to learn to read and write? Does this mean taking our eye off the acquisition of literacy and numeracy, assuming that

---

8   Bill Lucas and Guy Claxton, *Wider Skills for Learning: What Are They, How Can They Be Cultivated, How Could They Be Measured and Why Are They Important for Innovation?* (London: NESTA, 2009). Available at: http://www.nesta.org.uk/sites/default/files/wider_skills_for_learning_report.pdf.

children don't need any knowledge, and neglecting the elegance of algebra and the insight of Shakespeare? Absolutely not. Children need interesting, engaging and important things to learn *about*. But there is more to school than knowledge. Attitudes and beliefs will be formed there that will influence, for good or ill, the rest of young people's lives. To ignore these layers of the curriculum is not hard-nosed but bone-headed.

Is this an ill-conceived experiment with the next generation? Are we suggesting they be used as guinea pigs for some new-fangled, untried, radical revolution in education? Manifestly not. The status quo, or the image of the 'good grammar school' of the past, is neither safe nor neutral. To focus our attention exclusively on such schools is wilfully to ignore all the bright, interesting youngsters who are dying to learn, for whom the grammar school model is neither available nor appropriate.

All the methods we are going to illustrate in the next two chapters are already in use in good schools, where children are well-behaved and getting good results. They are just not as widely spread and as widely known as they should be. There is good empirical evidence to trust and support these methods, and encourage their use. But we have to stand up to a few noisy people who are mired in the past, unconcerned (despite their protestations) about the education of all those who must, of necessity, fail to do well in traditional exams, and too lazy to get to grips with the detail of these new methods or to read the research that supports them.

Chapter 4

What's worth learning these days?

It is utterly false and cruelly arbitrary to put all the play and learning into childhood, all the work into middle age, and all the regrets into old age.

Margaret Mead

As far as we can see, there are three kinds of things that deserve to be in the school curriculum. We call them utilities, treasures and exercise-machines. *Utilities* are things which are self-evidently useful for young people to know or be able to do. They include being able to tie your shoelaces (if this is still essential since the invention of Velcro), tell the time, check your change, read a newspaper, a timetable and a good book, fill in a form, write a coherent letter, behave sensibly if you get lost, ride a bike, swim and so on. To read the newspaper, or join in a conversation, it is necessary not just to have mastered the skills of reading and speaking but also to have some knowledge and understanding about the world and current affairs.

Much of this information is picked up by children – as by adults – on the fly. Much learning happens by inferring what people must be talking about (assuming they are making sense), and we all get very good at doing this without any formal instruction. If we can't fill in the gaps in this way, we ask people to stop and explain. But understanding how a city works or what the rules of football are, in a more systematic way, is also useful. To become informed and effective citizens, young people need to know something about, for example, the global financial crisis, climate change, neuroscience, sectarian violence, how it is possible for people to be 'groomed' or 'radicalised', the pros and cons of different forms of government and how the idea of the nation state is changing in an era of globalisation. We can argue about the detail, the ages at which each of the utilities should be introduced, and how to tell when they have been mastered to a good enough level, but the value of teaching or coaching things that are genuinely practical and useful in their own right is, in principle, pretty obvious.

Then there are *treasures*: things which we all agree may not be directly useful, in a rather utilitarian sense, but which, we broadly agree, form such an important part of our (however we define 'our') cultural heritage that everyone who lives here should have encountered them. This is much more contentious, because there are strong opinions but no practical touchstones against which to assess competing claims for inclusion. The traditional curriculum has been largely built around the discussion of treasures: discussions that have often become dull and formulaic under the pressure of traditional exams. There are also unintended consequences when selections of content are made on the basis of tradition and inertia, or in terms of the traditional cultural interests and values of one subset of the population. There is nothing inherently wrong with making children from Somalia, Romania or Pakistan study *Twelfth Night* or *Wuthering Heights*, if we agree that everyone who lives here should have encountered them, but the price is often that this exposure functions not as a lure for further appreciation of British culture, but an inoculation against it. A disagreeable dose of Shakespeare at school may stop you ever contracting Shakespeare again.

Selecting these treasures involves complex issues about which all of us have strong feelings – and traditional education doesn't like it when things get heated. It tries to organise the curriculum so that things are kept cool. In a multicultural society, there are going to be many different histories and beliefs at play, even in a primary school. But if we avoid such discussions, children are not going to learn how to address differences in an open-minded and respectful way, and the curriculum itself becomes populated with dull topics about which nobody cares enough to disagree. Few (except perhaps the odd Trad) can get terribly worked up about relative clauses or the difference between ionic and covalent bonding, so some schools spend a lot of time on those and not much on the rise of Islamic State or child sexual exploitation.

Finally there are *exercise-machines*. Topics and activities can justify their place in the curriculum, even if they are not utilities or treasures themselves, if studying them, in a particular way, does develop something that is useful. For example, learning to add fractions has become neither particularly useful (when was the last time you needed to?) nor, to many people's thinking, intrinsically valuable enough to count as a treasure. Children are growing up in a decimal and binary world, and while it may be useful to know what a third is in decimals, weeks spent laboriously trying to get bemused children to understand why ½ + ⅓ does not equal ⅖ could well have been spent more usefully. Unless, in the process of wrestling with the fractions, the children are developing some other capacity or habit that *is* useful – perseverance, patience or their powers of logical analysis, perhaps.

But, if this justification is to be used, we will want to know exactly what the target capability is, how adding fractions is going to be used to develop that capability (i.e. what activities will turn it from a pointless drag into a meaningful form of mental exercise), whether adding fractions is the most effective exercise-machine for developing that capability there is, and what the evidence is that the capability does, in fact, generalise to other contexts and materials. Could it not have been exercised even better by getting the children to spend half an hour each morning doing Sudoku? It's an empirical question, and the onus is on those who would defend the compulsory teaching of fractions (or the Tudors, or French irregular verbs) to present the evidence. With so many important and interesting things to be learned, jostling for time in the curriculum, such hard questions have to be asked. Strident assertions of value are not good enough. You could argue that adding fractions is only seen as a cultural treasure *because* of its long-standing, privileged place in the school curriculum, not the other way round. It's truly a sabre-toothed topic.

If you are as bemused as your children and pupils about the point of learning some of the things that are still on the curriculum (as they were in our day), take heart. Asking schools (and ministries) to justify them is an absolutely valid and important thing to do. We have heard of one brave school where every term the children are each given a 'joker' they can play at any point of any lesson during that term. When they do so, the teacher has to stop teaching and try to give the class their best explanation of why that topic is important enough to be taking up the children's time. The explanations are listened to respectfully and evaluated by the class. Trads might well be appalled by this apparent show of disrespect or lack of trust. Mods, however, will be open to the possibility that the thinking involved, and the discussion that could ensue, is a better preparation for life than passively accepting what you are told. This is not an opportunity to be 'cheeky' or 'disruptive' but to learn to be a more active and critical – in the best sense – consumer of your education.

Do you think school is teaching us how to think for ourselves? No. School teaches you how to answer how other people want you to answer. It's not about *your* thinking, it's just about giving the right answer to get the marks. If you think about it differently it's just wrong straight up. Have to do it their way 'cause otherwise you lose loads of marks. It's teaching people that life is 'one dimensional'.

Adam, Year 11, London secondary school

They definitely close your mind more than open it. Learning is actually a really powerful thing, but when you are taught like that, learning feels like a bad thing; you don't want to do it.

Chloe, recently left school

The purpose of school is to give people the tools and skills to think for themselves, and to engage with the people and ideas around them ... But by A levels, all of the teachers were reading us the notes, telling us what to write in our essays, and then marking them. In the upper school it was all about being analytical in exactly the right way to pass the exam.

Josh, recently left a state school

Bones of a 21st century curriculum

We are going to make some suggestions about what a curriculum for this century might be like. Please take these as illustrative, not definitive – and certainly not exhaustive. We will divide our remarks into six age groups, using the current English key stages (KS). Again, these are only rough suggestions of age-appropriateness for various goals; often children will be grouped not by age but by the stage of their developing expertise and understanding. KS0, or the early years foundation stage (EYFS), concerns young children from 3 to 5 years old; KS1 corresponds to Years 1 and 2 in primary school, and KS2 to Years 3–6; KS3 covers the first three years of secondary school, Years 7–9; KS4 covers the two years, 10 and 11, currently leading up to the GCSE exams; and KS5 is old-fashioned sixth form, Years 12 and 13, currently leading up to A levels.

Before we make some brief suggestions about what the central job of each of these stages might be, we need to make a preliminary point about project work, also known as problem-based or enquiry-based learning. We think that this approach, done well, is vital for three reasons: (1) for getting children's engagement in learning, (2) for accelerating their conventional achievement, and (3) for developing the habits of mind which we think should be at the core of education. The 'done well' is vital. It is as possible to do project-based learning badly as it is to do chalk-and-talk badly. Neither method by itself guarantees success; it all depends, as with so much in life, on how you do it. We will illustrate what 'done well' looks like as we work our way through the stages.

Be warned, though, that the Trads will start huffing and puffing at the very mention of projects. They think that project work means throwing children in at the deep end of unstructured, unsupervised learning, which is often way beyond their capabilities, and letting them drown. Their straw man is what they call 'minimally guided' project work, in which the teacher just does a whole lot less than they 'ought' to be doing, so they like to quote a research paper by Paul Kirschner and colleagues which finds that minimally guided project work doesn't work.[1] But that's just ill-thought-out project work, quite untypical of what you will find in most schools. Between 'laissez-faire' and 'total teacher control' there are hundreds of ways in which guidance is provided, and varied judiciously, *and* children are more engaged, independent and inquisitive than in the old-fashioned schoolroom. We go into lots of schools, and that is what we usually find. Trads tend not to go into schools much (or not schools other than their own) because the

---

1 Paul Kirschner, John Sweller and Richard Clark, Why minimal guidance during instruction does not work: an analysis of the failure of constructivist, discovery, problem-based, experiential, and inquiry-based teaching, *Educational Psychologist* 41(2) (2006): 75–86. Available at: http://www.cogtech.usc.edu/publications/kirschner_Sweller_Clark.pdf.

complexity and sophistication of what they might see would muck up their tidy oppositions.

Age 3 to 5 – EYFS: Serious play

Currently in England there are four guiding principles that underpin the early years foundation stage:

1. Every child is a unique child, who is constantly learning and can be resilient, capable, confident and self-assured.

2. Children learn to be strong and independent through positive relationships.

3. Children learn and develop well in enabling environments, in which their experiences respond to their individual needs and there is a strong partnership between practitioners and parents and/or carers.

4. Children develop and learn in different ways and at different rates.[2]

Nothing wrong with all of that, but the current framework goes on to make the EYFS sound very like 'pre-school'; that is, there is lots of emphasis on literacy and maths, and lots of assessments that children are expected to reach at different ages. We much prefer the less micro-managed specification that the EYFS originally had. The earlier

2 Department for Education, *Statutory Framework for the Early Years Foundation Stage: Setting the Standards for Learning, Development and Care for Children from Birth to Five* (Runcorn: DfE, 2012). Available at: https://www.gov.uk/government/uploads/system/uploads/attachment_data/file/271631/eyfs_statutory_framework_march_2012.pdf.

guidance stated that through well-planned play, both indoors and outdoors, children can:

- Explore, develop and represent learning experiences that help them make sense of the world.

- Practise and build up ideas, concepts and skills.

- Learn how to control impulses and understand the need for rules.

- Be alone, be alongside others or cooperate as they talk or rehearse their feelings.

- Take risks and make mistakes.

- Think creatively and imaginatively.

- Communicate with others as they investigate or solve problems.

- Express fears or relive anxious experiences in controlled and safe situations.[3]

This sounds as if it was written by people who knew and liked small children, and we would like to see it back. Note that it is not afraid to use the word 'play', because the writers do not oppose 'play' to 'serious learning'. It is much closer to the globally respected and widely copied early years curriculum from New Zealand called Te Whāriki, which means a woven mat in Maori. The image suggests that content and process are woven together; skills and attitudes develop

---

3 Department for Children, Schools and Families, *Practice Guidance for the Early Years Foundation Stage: Setting the Standards for Learning, Development and Care for Children from Birth to Five* (Nottingham: DCSF, 2008). Available at: http://webarchive.nationalarchives.gov.uk/20130401151715/https:/www.education.gov.uk/publications/eOrderingDownload/DCSF-00266-2008.pdf.

alongside knowledge and understanding as children work on interesting challenges and subject matter.

Age 5 to 7 – Key Stage 1: Growth mindsets for success and collaborative learning

In Chapter 2, we introduced you to some important research by Carol Dweck about how what we believe about ourselves really matters. Dweck, you will remember, has shown that there are two kinds of learners, those who have a fixed mindset and those she describes as having a growth mindset. Fixed mindset learners like to *prove* what they can do and tend to be averse to risk (you might look stupid) and hard work (struggling means you aren't very bright). Growth mindset children are all about *improving* what they can do. They don't mind in the least that, in the course of getting better at things, they make mistakes, struggle and don't look good. Babies are born with a growth mindset. By the time they start school, many children have already started to value looking good over finding out. It is vital that we make sure that children retain, or regain, their membership of the second of these two groups.

Exactly what subject or subjects children might be studying – the specific exercise-machines that will help them to develop self-belief, the ability to keep persisting with tricky questions and a willingness to practise and try things out – is, we believe, a matter for schools to determine. It's important that teachers help all children to feel that getting something wrong is not a cause for embarrassment, but an opportunity for learning and development. A 'mistake of the week' accompanied by an explicit attempt to tease out the insights it can bring the class is an example of the kind of curriculum we think children of this age need. And experiencing the satisfaction of 'getting it right' is crucial too.

At the same time, it is important that children learn to think, play and compete with each other. In the real world much of what we do requires us to collaborate. But it isn't easy. You have to learn to listen; to see that other people have different perspectives; to wait your turn and find out how to jump in skilfully and respectfully; to disagree graciously; to keep track of different threads and participants in the conversation. One of the reasons that learning in groups in schools can be ineffective is simply that the children have never been shown how to work in groups! Between the ages of 5 and 7 they can begin to practise different roles – coordinator, timekeeper, ideas person, fact-checker, planner and so on. Some schools use the popular technique known as Six Thinking Hats, created by Edward de Bono, as a basis for making switching roles fun (the children wear different coloured hats to signal which 'mode' they are currently in).[4] But while we like this approach for its creativity, we suggest that the give and take of working and learning together is so fundamental that it needs to imbue more of primary school life so that the habits of reading the moods of others, progress-checking and constructively giving and receiving feedback become deeply embedded.

Of course, children at this age also need to be well-grounded in the basics of number and words, but by far the most important things are that, by the time they are 8, they will have acquired the habit of reading and writing for

---

4   See http://www.debonogroup.com/six_thinking_hats.php.

pleasure, discovered the power of stories, and begun to develop a fascination for numbers and the extraordinary patterns and connections they bring with them. At the same time, as proto-scientists, artists, engineers and inventors, they will have needed lots of practical opportunities to make things. They will also have begun to understand that their bodies need to be looked after (in terms of diet and exercise and their interaction with other little bodies!).

A few years ago we worked with a teacher in a school in Milton Keynes who undertook some research into ways of making reading and writing fun for her Year 1 children in 'Elephants' class. The teacher chose *Green Eggs and Ham* by Dr Seuss as a book to read together (a good choice given its central character is Sam-I-Am who is reluctant to try things out but gradually learns to 'give it a go'). She equipped the Elephants with paper, pencils and clipboards and asked them where they'd like to do their writing. They chose to try in the classroom with the lights off and powered by torches, in the staffroom (achieved after a bit of negotiation!), lying on the floor in the library, in the school grounds and even in the local park. This simple but imaginative approach worked well. Accompanied by the normal phonics and handwriting practice, the confidence of the Elephants class increased, the teacher told us, as did the fluency and skill of their writing.

Another similarly adventurous example which we liked was the decision by teachers at Coombes School, in Berkshire, to teach the Great Fire of London by having the whole school (and parent body) construct a scale model of London outside in the grounds, then to orientate it so that the wind was blowing in the same direction as it was on that fateful day, then to light it in Thomas Farynor's bakery and see what happened. The children and assembled throng of parents potentially learned as much about the passage of fire as they did about the fragility of a capital city largely built of wood. The whole thing was filmed so that the learning could endure beyond the few minutes of the playground conflagration.[5]

There are two simple truths about learning that seem to escape the odd Trad. The first is that children learn best when they are fully engaged with what they are doing. For this to happen they have to be interested; to *want* to be able to do something that they can't yet do. The second truth is that they mostly want to do things that older people around them obviously enjoy doing, whether it be kicking a ball, reading a book or telling jokes. So they need to be surrounded by people they like who, for example, frequently and visibly read books for pleasure. And through this and other smart methods, they need to be coaxed to *want* to master things, not to be afraid of not doing so. Fear prevents you from locking your attention on to what you are doing – and that obviously slows learning down. The worst thing you can do with a child who is slow to read is to turn him into a 'problem', because being a problem makes you anxious and upset, and that stops you concentrating and trying. It's not rocket science!

---

5 You can read about this in one of the thought-provoking books by Learning through Landscapes: Jacqui Dean, *History in the School Grounds* (Winchester: Learning through Landscapes, 1999).

Age 7 to 11 – Key Stage 2: Projects driven by interest

Key Stage 2 will need to continue the apprenticeships in reading, writing and calculating, but we think that there could be two other strands. The first would involve a series of projects that are principally driven by interest in topics and questions that are intrinsically interesting to children of this age. Here's a lovely example about the Blackawton bees:

On 22 December 2010, the prestigious science journal, *Biology Letters*, produced by the Royal Society, published a paper entitled 'Colour and spatial relationships in bees'.[6] The paper reports an experiment which showed that bees could use an intricate synthesis of colour and pattern information to select the most pollen-laden flowers. The paper has 30 authors, 25 of whom are 8 to 10 years old. Three are teachers, one is a researcher and the lead author, P. S. Blackawton, is the name of their school, Blackawton Primary School. The experiment was initiated, designed, conducted and written up by the children (with a small amount of help). They described their 'principal finding' like this: "We discovered that bumble-bees can use a combination of colour and spatial relationships in deciding which colour of flower to forage from. We also discovered that science is cool and fun because you get to do stuff that no one has ever done before."

The researcher, Dr Beau Lotto of University College London, notes in his introduction to the published paper:

---

6 P. S. Blackawton, S. Airzee, A. Allen, et al., Colour and spatial relationships in bees, *Biology Letters* 7(2) (2011): 168–172.

The process of science is little different from the deeply resonant, natural processes of play. Play enables us to discover and create relationships and patterns ... This is science: the process that enables one to reveal previously unseen patterns of relationship ... But, because the outcome of all such [enquiry] is unpredictable, supporting this 'messyness', which is the engine of science, is critical to good science education (and indeed creative education generally) ... We have learned that doing 'real science' can stimulate tremendous interest in children in understanding the processes by which we make sense of the world.

Knowing more about bees is not the point. Knowing how bees find flowers is not useful for all children, and nor does this knowledge have a stronger claim to be an essential treasure than a million other facts and ideas. But studying bees captured these children's interest, and with some guidance they were able to use this study as an exercise-machine to learn truly valuable skills and insights about the processes of enquiry and discovery. They stretched their abilities to notice carefully, to collaborate, to record observations, to reason and draw conclusions, to refine technique, to communicate their findings and to deeply enjoy this learning. They are not just learning skills; they are strengthening their dispositions to learn in disciplined ways.

Nor is getting their findings published in a prestigious journal the point – though it must surely have given those children great pride and a huge amount of encouragement to pursue such enquiries still further. In their desire to work with a real scientist, to create new knowledge and 'do stuff that no one has ever done before', they fully commit their intelligence and stretch their learning power in the process.

Surely, only the most unreconstructed of Trads would prefer these children to be sitting obediently in rows, reciting their times tables (though they can certainly do that as well, if it is effective and enjoyable). Two researchers, Ann Brown at the University of Berkeley, California[7] and Chris Watkins at the Institute of Education in London,[8] have shown how, by deliberately seeking to set up classrooms as communities of enquiry, the level of understanding and quality of questioning becomes much deeper. Whether by teaching children how to function in a research team or through a technique known as 'jigsaw', it is possible to take young learners to the next level in their journey to becoming really effective learners. (Jigsaw learning organises large enquiries into component sub-tasks to be carried out by different groups, and then requires each group to collaborate with the others. A simple example would be writing, designing, printing and distributing a class newspaper which will call on groups to take on the different interdependent functions of a real newspaper.)

Sugata Mitra, who we introduced in Chapter 2, would have us go one stage further. He believes we should set up what he calls Self-Organised Learning Environments (SOLE) where children can work in groups, accessing the internet and other software, following up on a class project or taking them where their interests lead them. Mitra's research shows that this self-organised enquiry works

---

7   See Ann Brown and Joseph Campione, Guided discovery in a community of learners. In K. McGilly (ed.), *Classroom Lessons: Integrating Cognitive Theory and Classroom Practice* (Cambridge, MA: MIT Press/Bradford Books, 1994), pp. 229–270.

8   See Chris Watkins, *Classrooms as Learning Communities: What's In It for Schools?* (Abingdon: Routledge, 2005).

brilliantly – unless interrupted by adults. The world is divided as to whether this is a brilliant idea or a supreme act of folly. Trads hate it, Roms would love it and Mods like us think that we should be bold enough to try versions of SOLE from time to time and monitor its effects on the children. You can make up your own mind by googling the many descriptions of Mitra's work.

The other strand that should begin in KS2 is an introduction to the vast number of ways which grown-ups find of making a satisfying living. Some children develop unconsciously very limited – and limiting – ideas about what they could be: what they could dare or hope or aspire to be. Even casual remarks can close off an avenue: "Oh, that's not for me – or for people like me," "I could never do that," "That's not a feminine or manly thing to do so I'll cross it off the list of possibilities." From age 7 onwards, we think schools should be beginning to seed young minds with all sorts of possibilities, so children can see that 'people like me' do ten thousand different kinds of things to make a living, and have happy, fulfilled, responsible lives. Many parents and members of a school community talk well about their job, and a quick presentation followed by lots of questions is a good way of sparking children's interest. After-school clubs run by specialists tend to be even more effective as they develop longer term relationships and tend to involve children in real-world activities together relating to the target vocation.

Age 11 to 14 – Key Stage 3:
Real-world enquiries and possible selves

As pupils begin their secondary career, we envisage project work of diverse kinds, some designed by teachers to stretch certain learning habits of mind (there is an example of this in Chapter 5) and some designed largely by the students in response, this time, not just to personal interest but to some 'commissions' from the local community. Students, working in teams, provide genuine consultancy and research in response to issues that might be vexing local people. For example, they could include concerns arising from proposed housing developments, where the students research the likely implication of the development for local wildlife, road usage (e.g. parking, traffic jams, rat-runs) or increased pressure on local amenities such as sports facilities, doctors' surgeries and schools. Again, skills of enquiry, interviewing, data analysis and presentation will all be stretched and developed.

At primary school we would hope that all children will have understood deeply that being a 'good person' and a 'good learner' are themselves learnable. By the time they get to secondary school they will already be well on the way towards developing these habits. It should have become second nature to own up to a breakage or to finding lost property, to behave kindly towards new arrivals in the school, to be able to stay focused on a task despite some distractions, to listen carefully to others in a group, to persist in the face of difficulty and so on. In thousands of schools around the world, pupils may have encountered this 'habit-building' way of teaching in the guise of Building Learning Power (many of our examples are taken from this approach) or from other approaches with similar philosophies.[9] At some stage, no later than Key Stage 3, it is especially helpful if the techniques and attitudes of the 'powerful learner' are made explicit so that they are widely coached and discussed across the curriculum. Children are being helped to learn how to learn. There are many different ways of doing this, and all we would want to suggest here is that schools bear in mind two things.

First, they need to be sure that the approaches adopted should be well-researched. (In the 1990s, an approach called Brain Gym was much touted as the key to successful learning. It isn't. Teachers were told that children had fixed learning styles which they had to attend to if they were to learn well. They don't. It also briefly became fashionable to think that children exposed to the music of Mozart, ideally as early as possible in their lives, would become better mathematicians. They won't, although some may end up liking or hating the music!) Some people believed that you had to make children sip water all the time or their brains would dry up and learning would stop. It doesn't.

Second, the focus of these learning habits needs to be embedded in the whole curriculum, and not administered as a stand alone module. It doesn't work to see learning to learn as a kind of occasional booster injection of learning to

9   Building Learning Power (BLP) is a programme inspired by Guy which explicitly helps young people to become better learners, both in school and out. It helps schools to create a culture that systematically cultivates habits and attitudes that enable young people to face difficulty and uncertainty calmly, confidently and creatively. For examples of schools putting BLP ideas into practice, see Guy Claxton, Maryl Chambers, Graham Powell and Bill Lucas, *The Learning Powered School: Pioneering 21st Century Education* (Bristol: TLO, 2011). For more general information about the underpinning research and practices, see www.buildinglearningpower.co.uk.

learn capabilities. We know from various research that, when this happens, learning to learn does not transfer into the various subjects where it needs to be applied, nor to out-of-school life, and it often becomes marginalised as an activity.

Learning to learn has helped me to learn better with other people. When working in a group I think about what we have done in the lesson and get my ideas straight, and I find that helps me tolerate anything! I can work in a group with anyone now without blowing my top! It definitely helps me, even at home.

Jake, Year 7

KS3 should also build on the exposure to a wide range of occupations and 'possible selves' begun at KS2. Once upon a time there used to be lots of people in schools called 'careers officers' who were skilled in knowing which educational pathways might work for which child. These days such people are very thin on the ground. There are also so many courses on offer at college and university that it is nigh on impossible for any teacher to keep abreast of them.

Luckily there is a great website called www.icould.com which shows short film-clips of all kinds of people talking about the journeys that led them to the work (whether employed or self-employed) they now love doing. Just play the students one of these every morning, and who knows, maybe a seed of a possibility, a glimmer of an idea, might be sown. And maybe even start offering small 'work experience' opportunities to the children that they can report back on, or make their own 'icould' videos for the rest of the school to see.

I had a really good history teacher, fun and full of energy. He taught us in a different way. Once before school he asked me, "Hannah, in the middle of the lesson can you keep on asking questions and I'll ignore you, then you storm out?" So I was like, yeah. The lesson was about reliable sources, so after I stormed out he made everyone write a letter to the head teacher explaining what had happened. Then he called me back in and told everyone it was a set-up. We read all the letters out and some, of course, were really biased – my best friends vs. people who hated me, kind of thing. It was a really clever way to *show* us what we were learning about.

Hannah, Year 9, London secondary school

Age 14 to 16 – Key Stage 4: Sustained engagement with bodies of knowledge and research

We suggest that at this stage students bring their already well-developed reading, writing, collaborating and researching habits to bear on matters of national and global significance. In so doing they would be required to engage with the disciplined bodies of knowledge and research that inform these issues. The goal is for all young people to develop, as much as they can, a rigorous understanding of these issues, with all their complexities and controversies, which will enable them to play an informed part in public debates.

Key Stage 4 would thus provide a means to develop a kind of 'intermediate literacy' – an ability to read good quality literature, and to convey it fluently – that sits between the superficial opinions of, for example, tabloid newspapers and the technical world of research journals. In every school subject there is a progression across the key stages, not just of vocabulary but also of the intricacy and abstraction of arguments and ideas, and it is this 'literacy of thought' that students of this age are ready to focus on. (In KS2 you can set up a simple experiment and ask the children, "What do you think is going to happen?" You can't ask that about the periodic table.) Many pupils never become fluent in this more abstract-but-precise way of thinking and writing, and nor do they master the art of sliding between the language of concrete, personally felt experience and the abstract languages of academic research – but they could, and it would be socially highly useful for them to do so.[10]

For example, people tend to fall into two groups when you ask them about the causes of the global financial crisis of 2008. About 80% of people blame venal or stupid individuals ('villains' or 'idiots', basically). They take a rather moralistic and simplistic stance. The other 20% take a more systemic view; they talk about the nature of institutions, their cultures and fallibilities, and the way they interact.[11] This one-fifth of the adult population turns out to be significantly better educated than the rest. They are able to take

10 See Peter Freebody, Eveline Chan and Georgina Barton, Curriculum as literate practice: language and knowledge in the classroom. In Kathy Hall, Teresa Cremin, Barbara Comber and Luis Moll (eds), *International Handbook of Research on Children's Literacy, Learning, and Culture* (Oxford: Wiley-Blackwell, 2013), pp. 304–318.

11 See David Leiser, Sacha Bourgeois-Gironde and Rinal Benita, Human foibles or system failure: lay perceptions of the 2008–9 financial crisis, *Journal of Socio-Economics* 17 (2010): 2–39.

a less emotive or self-righteous view of the situation, and thus arrive at more penetrating analyses, and potentially more effective solutions. They are better at what has come to be called 'systems thinking'. Wouldn't it be good (for all of us except climate deniers and the oil industry) if thousands of 16-year-olds were flooding out of schools well-informed and eloquent about such matters? About climate change (or what James Lovelock now insists on calling 'global heating')? About the relationship between the arbitrary carving up of areas of Central Europe, Africa and Asia by old colonial powers, and the resurgence of tribalism, whether ethnic, religious or geographical, in those areas once oppressive rule begins to crack? About the exposure of previously hidden experiences of war or abuse through literature, art and film? This is not a left-wing, anti-establishment agenda; it is a depth-of-understanding-of-complex-issues agenda. And if that is not a legitimate purpose of education, we don't know what is.

There are many high quality, well-written, contemporary non-fiction books that could serve as the basis for the discussion and development of this ability to bring good information, theory and argument into the arena of public debate. Kindle and paperback editions are not expensive. On the financial crisis, 15-year-olds could read John Lanchester's *Whoops! Why Everyone Owes Everyone and No One Can Pay* or John Coates' brilliant exposition of the neuroscience of risk-taking, *Between the Hour of Dog and Wolf*.[12] On climate change, George Monbiot's *Heat: How to Stop the Planet Burning* or James Lovelock's *The Revenge of Gaia* would be

---

12 John Lanchester, *Whoops! Why Everyone Owes Everyone and No One Can Pay* (London: Penguin, 2010); John Coates, *Between the Hour of Dog and Wolf: Risk-Taking, Gut Feelings and the Biology of Boom and Bust* (London: Fourth Estate, 2012).

good.[13] On the evolution and future of humankind, anything by Richard Dawkins is an exemplary piece of science
writing, while Jared Diamond's *The Third Chimpanzee* is a
great read[14] – there is even a version adapted to the reading
level of 10-year-olds now on the market, so such reading
could start even earlier.

In understanding recent developments in psychology,
David Brooks' *The Social Animal*, Daniel Kahneman's *Thinking
Fast and Slow* and Jonathan Haidt's *The Righteous Mind* are
highly accessible, well-researched and very thought-provoking.[15] Alexander Diener and Joshua Hagen's *Borders: A Very
Short Introduction* brings history and politics together in a way
that illuminates many current post-colonial conflicts.[16] Many
works of fiction also address contemporary or historical
issues of real importance in lively ways – for example, John
le Carré's *The Constant Gardener* or Hilary Mantel's *Wolf Hall*
and *Bring Up the Bodies*.[17] Any would-be writer of fiction
would learn hugely from John Yorke's *Into the Woods: How
Stories Work and Why We Tell Them*.[18] Olivia Fane's *The
Conversations: 66 Reasons to Start Talking* would be a terrific

13 George Monbiot, *Heat: How to Stop the Planet Burning* (London: Penguin,
2007); James Lovelock, *The Revenge of Gaia* (London: Penguin, 2007).

14 Jared Diamond, *The Third Chimpanzee* (London: Harper Perennial, 2007).

15 David Brooks, *The Social Animal* (London: Short Books, 2012); Daniel
Kahneman, *Thinking Fast and Slow* (London: Penguin, 2012); Jonathan
Haidt, *The Righteous Mind: Why Good People are Divided by Politics and Religion*
(London: Allen Lane, 2012).

16 Alexander Diener and Joshua Hagen, *Borders: A Very Short Introduction* (New
York: Oxford University Press, 2012).

17 John le Carré, *The Constant Gardener* (London: Hodder, 2005); Hilary
Mantel, *Wolf Hall* (London: Fourth Estate, 2010) and *Bring Up the Bodies*
(London: Fourth Estate, 2013).

18 John Yorke, *Into the Woods: How Stories Work and Why We Tell Them*
(London: Penguin, 2014).

primer for debates about painful contemporary issues.[19] Students could read these books as a kind of 'book club', meeting weekly to discuss a chapter, and having regular 'flipped' sessions with their teacher to ask questions and iron out misunderstandings and disagreements. As a group, having to read a whole book and master complex arguments would clearly stretch a host of valuable capabilities: reading, concentration, discussion, resilience and imagination, just for starters. And, of course, there are various online interpretations and e-versions of the books which could be explored.

Age 16 to 19 – Key Stage 5: Deep scholarship and extended making

Here we envisage two strands: one vocational and the other philosophical. Having explored a whole variety of vocational options and 'possible selves' earlier in their school careers, the vocational strand could require a commitment to following one or two vocational pathways in more detail, in a mixture of disciplinary learning and internships or apprenticeships. By vocational here we mean to do with any likely future career, be it in medicine, web design, social work, catering, teaching or sport. We think that vocational should apply to the developing work identities of all young people, not just those who are not cut out for more disembodied kinds of study. And, by the same token, all young people should be developing a base of knowledge and

---

19 Olivia Fane, *The Conversations: 66 Reasons to Start Talking* (London: Square Peg, 2013).

understanding that enables them to be thoughtful rather than mechanical practitioners. (As we all know, it is possible to be a well-informed, thoughtful and creative plumber, and a mediocre, mechanical lecturer, GP or solicitor. Creative intelligence is not the province of a small sector of the job market – and nor is absent-minded or sloppy thinking!)

We think that the more general and philosophical component of KS5 could well be derived from something like the International Baccalaureate (IB). It should really stretch students to think about complex issues of current relevance and concern. This is the core of the IB diploma:

- An *extended essay* asks students to engage in independent research through an in-depth study of a question relating to one of the subjects they are studying. The 'world studies' extended essay option allows students to focus on a topic of global significance which they examine through the lens of at least two of their subjects.

- The *theory of knowledge (TOK)* course develops a coherent approach to learning that unifies the academic disciplines. In this course on critical thinking, students enquire into the nature of knowing and deepen their understanding of knowledge as a human construction.

- *Creativity, action, service (CAS)* involves students in a range of activities alongside their academic studies throughout the diploma programme. Creativity encourages students to engage in the arts and creative thinking. Action seeks to develop a healthy lifestyle through physical activity. Service with the community offers a vehicle for new learning with academic value. The three strands of CAS enhance students' personal and interpersonal development through experiential learning and enable journeys of self-discovery.

We would like to add an *extended physical project* to balance the extended essay. Students would be required to make something beautiful and present it to an audience. It could be a piece of furniture or a bowl, a gymnastics display or a dance, a sculpture, painting or digital installation, a book of poetry or a storybook for younger children, a four-course meal or dozens of other technically accomplished outputs. Either separately or in conjunction with this, we would like to see a *collaborative project* too, in which the honours and responsibilities are shared – as indeed they are in much of 'real life'.

The theory of knowledge course should provide an essential – and challenging – corrective to the preceding years of acquiring specific bundles of knowledge, skill, attitude and understanding.[20] Its input should be composed solely of provocations to simplistic ideas about knowledge, learning and the composition of the mind. Any lingering attachment to ideas and beliefs, such as those below, could be challenged with visual illusions, moral dilemmas and paradoxes, and the classroom could resound with agonised discussion as students' minds get stretched and hitherto unquestioned certainties are put to the test.

- Knowledge is, in principle, secure and reliable.
- The Ten Commandments tell us what to do in any situation.

---

20 For a good introduction to theory of knowledge, see Eileen Dombrowski, John MacKenzie and Mike Clarke, *Perspectives on a curious subject: what is IB theory of knowledge all about?* IB Research Paper (2011).

- Intelligence is a fixed, general-purpose resource largely determined by our genes.

- Perception shows us the world as it really is.

- The mind is separate from the body.

- There is always a best solution to a tricky moral situation.

- Google has made teaching redundant.

- There is no such thing as society (only individual people).

- Creativity is the province of the arts.

The IB's own description of theory of knowledge speaks for itself:

The TOK course encourages critical thinking about knowledge itself. Its core content is questions like these: What counts as knowledge? How does it grow? What are its limits? Who owns knowledge? What is the value of knowledge? What are the implications of having, or not having, knowledge?

Students entering the Diploma Programme typically have 16 years of life experience and more than 10 years of formal education behind them. They have accumulated a vast amount of knowledge, beliefs and opinions from academic disciplines and their lives outside the classroom. In TOK they have the opportunity to step back from the relentless acquisition of new knowledge in order to consider knowledge issues. TOK activities and discussions aim to help students discover and express their views on knowledge issues. The course encourages students to share ideas with others and to listen to and learn from what others think. In this process students' thinking and their understanding of knowledge as a human construction are shaped, enriched and deepened.[21]

The ideas in this chapter are not intended to be remotely definitive. Rather, they are presented to start some different conversations about what we might want young people to learn at 5, 7, 9, 11, 14 and 19. Our intention is to populate the curriculum with challenges to think about, and to stretch young people's abilities to think, to critique, to communicate and to act effectively – not just to mug up bodies of received opinion simply in order to open a gate into the next field of learning. We want to bring knowing, thinking, feeling and acting back together, as a powerful launch pad for a thoughtful, responsible and adventurous life.

---

21 You can read more about the IB's TOK at: http://www.ibo.org/contentassets/0339a02316d742b7be8c358144ae9856/ibtokeng.pdf, as well as see a wider picture of its approach to learning.

Chapter 5

Reasons to be cheerful

The future is already here — it's just not very evenly distributed.

William Gibson

So far we've painted a picture of schools which may be rather different from the one with which you are familiar. If you are a teacher or parent you may have laughed (or cried) out loud at the gap between what we are imagining and the experience you are having of your children's school. Similarly, if you are reading this wearing your employer's hat you may be wondering if we are inhabiting the same world as you do, where job applicants regularly show an alarming lack of basic literacy and numeracy, or even basic aspects of self-organisation.

Or perhaps neither of these imaginary reactions is accurate. Maybe you know schools that *are* doing much of what we are talking about. Or perhaps you are an employer who has developed a great relationship with local schools and are in active discussions about how the kinds of broader attributes we describe can best be developed. Whatever your response, in this chapter we want to offer you hope; to show you that, as William Gibson suggests, if you look around, you can see many examples of the future of schooling, even if they are not yet locally available for you. Many of them are drawn from schools which have been using approaches to teaching and learning like BLP.

At school I used to be a good learner but now in my opinion I am a brilliant learner! I have found a part of me where I can just get on and do what I need to do. For example, I always check my work through. Even now I still make mistakes in my work but I edit it and it comes out a lot better than I thought it would. Since BLP I'm more patient, and I have learned that listening to other children helps me too.

Kieran, Year 6

BLP not only helps me, but it helps others around me. I have a little sister who is 4 years old and goes to a primary school without BLP. When I use phrases like, "What did you learn?" and "Did you use questioning?", that really helps her to understand what she is learning about and how it's helping her in other situations – not just the one she's in at school. When she's reading something she can now persevere if she doesn't understand, and if she doesn't understand a topic at school, she'll say, "Well, I have used … to overcome this situation." It helps you to become your own learner.

Victoria, Year 9

I used to get embarrassed and not like talking … BLP has opened new doors for me, it's made me more confident. Things like listening and empathy – now instead of getting embarrassed, I think of how other people react to things, and learn how I can react when I don't know something. I mentioned BLP to my friends at ski school, and then the whole week we were talking about how we had naturally used BLP. We were questioning what we could do better, looking for different techniques to improve our skiing, looking out for dangers. It's something to structure your life on, you use it every day.

Clara, Year 9

In this chapter we start by looking at some real examples of where the ideas we have been discussing are already being put into practice – where children are being systematically helped to build 21st century character and, at the same time, are getting better results than ever. We hope you'll see that there are many reasons to be optimistic. We just need to shout about them and use the examples they offer to encourage other schools to do similarly. We want you to feel inspired to go forth and multiply.

Pioneering schools

Miriam Lord Community School is a very large primary school in Bradford. It has high proportions of children for whom English is not their first language, and of those who are eligible for the pupil premium. Many children join the school with skills and knowledge that are well below the national average. In 2013 the inspectors put the school in a category called 'requires improvement'. In July 2014 they visited again, and now Miriam Lord is 'good with outstanding features'. Their report says: "The pupils are very keen to learn. They say that teachers 'make our tasks fun and challenging', and that 'the work can be a bit hard, but the hard bits make you learn new things – you don't learn when you don't have a challenge'."[1] The school has used the Building Learning Power framework to build this attitude quite deliberately. Here are some examples of what you might see and hear if you were to drop in to Miriam Lord.

The Year 2s are developing what they call their 'noticing muscles'. They have six questions that are guiding their learning:

1. Am I good at noticing details (e.g. similarities and differences between things)?

2. Do I want to know more about what we are studying?

3. Have I got a good question to ask?

4. How good am I at staying on task?

5. How good am I at concentrating on what I am doing despite distractions?

6. Am I interested in what I am doing?

In a maths lesson, the children are working with blocks of different lengths and colours to represent different numbers (you may know them as Cuisenaire rods). One boy, Arjan, is trying to represent the number 67 – he needs six tens-sticks to represent the 60, and then seven unit-cubes to make the 7. But under the 7 he has put seven tens-sticks. Instead of

---

1   Ofsted, Inspection Report: Miriam Lord Community Primary School (15–16 July 2014).

correcting him straight away, his teacher asks him to 'notice the details' of what he has done.

Arjan: I notice that I've put six tens-sticks under the 6.

Teacher: What do you notice?

Arjan: [points at the units column where he has put seven tens-sticks instead of seven unit-cubes] That I've got this bit wrong.

Teacher: Well, you've noticed something useful. What numbers did you make with the equipment?

Arjan: 60 and 70.

Teacher: So, now can you revise your answer?

Arjan changes the units column to correctly show 7 unit-cubes. His teacher asks him to explain what he now notices.

What do *you* notice about that little exchange? You may have been struck by the fact that Arjan does not get upset about having made a mistake; he just spots it and uses his observation to think how to correct it. He isn't just being helped to get the right answer (although he does); he is being coached to be more attentive to what he is doing, to think more clearly, to correct his own mistakes and not to get upset just because he didn't get it right first time. Cumulatively, this 'coaching' will make Arjan a better learner: more confident, enthusiastic and perceptive about his learning so he will learn faster and more effectively.

The Year 3s are getting toward the end of a unit focusing on 'How to live a healthy lifestyle', and to consolidate their learning they have been asked to plan and run a successful 'healthy cafe' to which their families will be invited. They are using a tool called the TASC wheel (Thinking

Actively in a Social Context), which was created by Belle Wallace.[2] The TASC wheel helps them orchestrate the task; their teacher is doing very little to guide or rescue them from the considerable difficulty of the assignment. Instead pupils respond to a series of helpful prompt questions such as:

- What do I know about this?

- What is the task?

- How many ideas can I think of?

- Which is the best idea?

- How well did I do?

- What have I learned?

The wheel provides a colourful and pupil-friendly way of structuring planning, thinking and progress.

The children set to work researching menu choices, budgeting the cost of various ingredients and designing and writing the invitations. They also design a questionnaire to gauge customer satisfaction with various aspects of their performance. Then they learn how to set the tables, prepare the food and drinks and, when their cafe opens its doors, gather orders from the 'customers', serve the different dishes, write out the 'bills', give them their change and dish out the questionnaires. After the event, they analyse the results from the questionnaires, and, as a whole class, use the information gleaned to reflect on their performance and to draw lessons for the future.

---

2 For a clear explanation of where TASC came from, see Belle Wallace, Teaching thinking and problem skills, *Educating Able Children* (Autumn 2000): 20–24. Available at: http://teachertools.londongt.org/en-GB/resources/Thinking_skills_b_wallace.pdf.

Bryan Harrison, the head teacher, wrote, "The event was well attended by parents who commented on how professional the event was, and how much confidence the children had shown. There were genuine moments of deep pride shared between the children and their families."

Nobody could do anything other than applaud this as a wonderful piece of education. The children are being stretched and are rising to a significant challenge. They are undaunted by this because their previous learning has cumulatively built up their capacity to cope and to be independent, resourceful and collaborative. They are using their maths and their English in meaningful ways that deepen their competence. They are learning to plan, reflect, make collective decisions and take responsibility – all habits that will benefit them in later life. They are utterly engaged and, at the end, bursting with pride at what they have managed to achieve. The community is involved and impressed. The parents see the growth in their children, and are totally supportive of the school. The children, let us remind you, are 7 and 8 years old.

Whether it is Blackawton bees or a healthy cafe doesn't matter. What does matter is that teachers are finding questions and creating challenges that engage children's interest and energy, and are skilled enough to structure the activities that follow in a way that systematically stretches valuable, transferable habits of mind. At Miriam Lord, the children are learning something really useful – to understand the basics of a healthy diet – *and* they are using this topic as an exercise-machine to drive the development of other, really useful attitudes and capabilities. What's not to like?

Further up the school, the Year 5s are studying the Amazon. All kinds of useful and interesting discussions and understandings can flow from this topic, and do: the different beliefs of indigenous peoples, the threat to wildlife, forests as 'the lungs of the world', the complex politics and economics of developing countries such as Brazil, and so on. But at Miriam Lord, this topic is also being used to develop more sophisticated learning habits and skills, such as internet research and note-taking. The children are given a text and challenged, both alone and in small groups, to distil out the key points (an ability that had been noted as underdeveloped in these children by an earlier assessment).

Within the topic there are a range of tasks that offer different degrees of challenge, and the children are encouraged to reflect on their own abilities in relation to the tasks, and select the ones that give their 'learning muscles the best stretch'. This not only gives the children a greater feeling of ownership and engagement, but also develops their ability to assess their current levels of understanding and ability for themselves. In a similar vein, children are encouraged to decide for themselves when to work on their own, when it would be better to join a group of other children and when they really need some help and guidance from the teacher. Over the course of the term, the children made 3D models of key features of the Amazon which the head teacher describes as 'stunning'. They wrote articles about some of the environmental issues and stretched their mathematical competence by working out rainfall averages and presented these in a variety of formats using ICT.

Any ideologically driven rhetoric about the inadequacies of project work, or the absurdity of 'expecting children to be experts', utterly fails to do justice to these sophisticated classrooms, and to the interwoven development of knowledge and understanding, technical skills and habits of mind, which is palpably taking place. There is no opposition between 'gaining knowledge' and 'learning to think'. They form a double helix. Knowledge deepens and broadens at the same time as the capacities to think, learn and be creative are being cultivated.

A few miles west of Bradford, across the Pennine Hills, lies the village of Barrowford, where the primary school has also made extensive use of BLP ideas. The school hit the headlines worldwide in July 2014 because the head teacher, Rachel Tomlinson, sent to every pupil in Year 6 a customised version of a letter that had originated in America. (Teachers – along with scientists and artists and athletes – are always borrowing and adapting each other's ideas; that's how good practice spreads.) Here is an extract from Rachel's letter:

Dear …

Please find enclosed your end of KS2 test results. We are very proud of you as you have demonstrated huge amounts of commitment and tried your very best during this tricky week.

However, we are concerned that these tests do not always assess all of what it is that make each of you special and unique. The people who create these tests and score them do not know each of you – the way your teachers do, the way I hope to, and certainly not the way your families do. They do not know that many of you speak two languages. They do not know that you can play a musical instrument or that you can dance or paint a picture. They do not know that your friends count on you to be there for them or that your laughter can brighten up the dreariest day. They do not know that you can write poetry or songs, play or participate in sports, wonder about the future, or that sometimes you take care of your little brother or sister after school ... They do not know that you can be trustworthy, kind or thoughtful, and that you try, every day, to be your very best ... The scores you get will tell you something but they will not tell you everything.

So enjoy your results and be very proud of these but remember there are many ways of being smart.

The letter went viral on the internet – because, we must presume, it rang a deep bell with millions of people. The letter praises the children for their achievement on conventional tests (the so-called Key Stage 2 SATs), and told them to be proud of their results and of their willingness to work hard and try their best. But it also reminded them of the other accomplishments and layers of their character that they should be proud of too: trustworthiness, diligence, cheerfulness, kindness, artistic flair.

There is nothing in the letter that could possibly be read as encouraging the children to devalue their education. However, Chris McGovern, chairman of the Campaign for Real Education, was quoted in the *Daily Mail* on 15 July as saying: "They're undermining confidence that the children may have in the education system. ... It's an indirect attack on the Government. The message that the school is sending to the children is that somehow they are being betrayed by the system. ... Schools should not be a platform for promoting political ideologies – they should be neutral."[3] Hmm,

3   Sarah Harris, There are many ways of being smart ... Headteacher writes to pupils saying not to worry about exams, *Daily Mail* (15 July 2014). Available at: http://www.dailymail.co.uk/news/article-2693045/Primary-school-headteachers-inspirational-letter-pupils-ahead-test-results-earns-praise-parents.html.

you have to work quite hard to see it that way. And you have to be rather uninquisitive, at the very least, to see why such dangerously seditious and anarchic extremism should appeal so strongly to millions of regular mums and dads.

Perhaps what is objectionable is not the temerity of mentioning the 95% of children's characters, accomplishments and interests that are ignored by much conventional education, but the very neglect of those qualities by so many schools. By the way, both the achievement of pupils and the quality of teaching at Barrowford was 'good' at the last Ofsted inspection, and the inspectors were moved to comment approvingly:

Spiritual, moral, social and cultural awareness is a strength of the school. The curriculum continuously reinforces positive attitudes towards learning and the development of skills and qualities such as perseverance, reasoning and empathy.[4]

How many times do we need to be told that the systematic development of positive learning dispositions is perfectly possible, and perfectly compatible with a commitment to literacy, numeracy and good test scores?

Being resilient has helped me try things; like, if I don't know a question in SATs I'll now have a go – and I might get it right! Also, if I don't have a pen or pencil or something, instead of sitting around waiting for one I'll go to the back of the classroom and get one! To start with I didn't like being asked to be reflective; I didn't see

4   Ofsted, Inspection Report: Barrowford School (11–12 September 2012).

the point. But now I understand that it's better to find your own mistakes, because then you'll never do it again. And being reflective has helped me write better stories with more detail that have all the good things in!

Hugo, Year 6

In Year 5 I wasn't very resourceful. I would come in in the morning and wait to be told what to do. Now I come in and get on with the task that is set. And BLP has taught me to check my work through and learn from my mistakes. When I play games I am not a sore loser any more; I just think about what I need to do to win next time. Overall I think BLP has had a massive effect on me.

Jake, Year 6

Before BLP I was never able to finish what I had started. Now I can finish my work, I pay attention more and I am not distracted any more. I notice more things – connections etc. – during the lesson. And before, I never asked questions and I never dreamed of trying to look for links between the topic and what I already knew. But now I ask more questions, get my resources sorted and basically don't fuss!

Elsie, Year 6

Let's stay in the north of England and travel back over the Pennines to North Shore Academy in Stockton-on-Tees. North Shore is a challenging secondary school. In January 2012 it was placed in Ofsted's lowest category, 'special measures'. The GCSE results that year were dire – just 22% of pupils achieved five good GCSEs including English and maths. A new principal, Bill Jordan, was brought in to turn things around – and he decided to continue with the work that his deputy, Lynn James, had already started to champion to build students' ownership of learning. They predicted, a year later, a GCSE success rate of 47%. In fact, 53% of students in 2013 hit that GCSE target. In the same year, three other local secondary schools, none with as tough a catchment area as North Shore, achieved 33%, 35% and 47%. This is an astonishing turnaround.

What is Bill and Lynn's philosophy? They have posted a list of the 'commitments' which North Shore now makes to all its students on their website. Here are two of them:

- Outstanding learning and teaching which engages pupils and is active, collaborative and encourages independence.

- Student voice intended to empower and involve young people in the development and delivery of their own education and the life of their academy.[5]

As school leaders, they have aimed to establish a culture of good behaviour, and then asked the teachers to develop their teaching so as to give the students progressively more independence and responsibility for their learning. To pull this off takes time and support, of course, and Lynn has asked BLP principal consultant Graham Powell to work with staff on a regular basis to help them shift their practice. To begin with, some of the teaching was spoon-feeding the students too much, and they had become used to adopting a rather

---

5   See www.northshoreacademy.org.uk/about/vision-values.

passive role in the classroom. In his early observations, Graham noted:

Students are compliant and attempt tasks set but their engagement is limited and teachers are the focus of attention for too long before setting them to work on their own. In too many lessons students comply but aren't encouraged to enjoy the struggle of learning which assures progress and engagement. Students are not always required to think sufficiently for themselves. Teachers do too much of the thinking for them. Teachers might make more use of activities that require students to ask questions of themselves, each other and the resources that are before them.

Over time, teachers have changed their ways, and now students have become more active in managing, researching, designing and evaluating learning for themselves and – though we are sure you don't need reminding – their results are rocketing up as well. In their latest Ofsted inspection, North Shore got a 'good' for teaching and learning. The report noted: "Since the last full inspection, the overall quality of teaching has improved significantly" and "Students … have good attitudes to learning."[6]

In various situations outside of school BLP has helped my thinking to be more logical and analytical. If I get lost I now think through all the possibilities of who to contact, how to contact them, where to go, why I would go to that place and how that would help me.

6   Ofsted, Inspection Report: North Shore Academy (12–13 December 2013).

Within school it helps you to persevere when you just want to give up! Recently, I had to produce an exact replica of a Picasso painting for DT homework. It took a *very* long time. I had to keep at it, until I got everything right – the proportion, the tone. BLP helped me with that, both consciously and subconsciously. When I finished it I felt really proud! And I set my standards really high!

Dominic, Year 8

Next, we come south to another comprehensive school, Goffs School, an academy in the stereotypically leafy Home Counties. Although the levels of achievement, and the nature of the students, are very different from North Shore, the journey that the teaching staff have been on over the last two or three years has been surprisingly similar. Nigel Appleyard, a history teacher who has been spearheading the development of BLP at Goffs, describes his own experience with his sixth-form class:

I started to provide them with stimulus material that would get them stuck. I wanted them to generate their own questions and explore possibilities for themselves. I was determined to make *them* do the thinking! At first I met with some resistance. One student in particular intimated that it was my job to teach the group and give them the answers that they could repeat in the exam to get the grades they needed. I explained to them that that way of teaching wasn't going to prepare them properly for the demands of the exam, or for their future needs.

I sensed that some of the group were not convinced. I didn't give in, and gradually they came to expect to be challenged in lessons and to rise to it. They started to get disappointed if I didn't set them something intriguing or problematic. Things have moved on, and they are much more actively engaged and now regularly involved in the planning and delivery of lessons. They have taken on responsibility for creating provocative, relevant and stimulating starter activities to 'warm up their learning muscles' and they lead the discussions that distil what they have learned and what they need to learn. They have become a different group: they have transformed themselves into students who no longer depend on me to provide them with all the answers.

And the exam results are improving year on year. In 2014, there was a 99% pass rate at A level, and the school's own target for A and A* grades at A level was exceeded by 11%!

At the school I'm in now, the economics teacher had walked out – so these kids were scheduled to have economics lessons, but without any teacher. I kind of adopted this class. I held back one guy at the end of the lesson and gave him a book to read. I put it in his hands, so that everyone could see. The next day, another student who's usually really nice was giving me a little bit of attitude. At the end of the lesson, everyone left but she kind of hopped around, and finally said, "I want a book too." And this is what I was going for to begin with. I, of course, had the exact book I wanted to give her. Over the next week, every one of my kids came in and asked for a book to read. So here are kids who are probably not going to pass the exam – most of my students have known their predicted grades of E and D for so long that they have no aspiration to go to uni – who are intellectually curious enough to want to be challenged.

Rob, economics teacher,
London secondary school

Our final example is Honywood Community Science School in Coggeshall, Essex. Its head teacher is a passionate advocate of using digital technology to give students more responsibility. They are encouraged, following clearly laid out schemes of work in maths, to plan their own learning pathways, and are coached in how to do this by higher level teaching assistants. There is also a library of high quality online resources. Honywood is a BYOD (bring your own device) school and students are expected to be able to switch between the online learning which they are leading and more traditional teacher-led instruction. Honywood does not follow any one approach to learning but has built its own well-thought-through approach called HonySkills.

HonySkills at Honywood

- Communicate in writing, orally, physically, graphically and by using ICT.

- Solve problems.

- Cooperate and collaborate with others.

- Analyse information and draw conclusions from it.

- Synthesise information, evaluate and form judgements about it.

- Empathise.

- Be creative.
- Gain the knowledge and skills to be healthy in body and mind.
- Persist when times are hard.
- Acquire the knowledge that valuing the struggle to learn will make you more successful.
- Think for yourself.
- Learn independently.
- Be competitive, never being content that you have done your best.
- Conceive of things in abstract as well as concrete form.
- Criticise constructively.
- Take responsibility for your learning and your life.

Head teacher Simon Mason is a driving force and a prolific communicator with his staff. Here is part of what he wrote as a guest blogger on the Expansive Education Network website.[7] (There's more on expansive education on page 135.)

As part of a new curriculum we introduced in September 2011, we have focused on sixteen skills, attitudes, dispositions and behaviours which we feel are essential for

7 We have created an alliance, the Expansive Education Network (www.expansiveeducation.net), and we have written a book telling the stories of schools across the world who are expansive educators: Bill Lucas, Guy Claxton and Ellen Spencer, *Expansive Education: Teaching Learners for the Real World* (Melbourne: Australian Council for Educational Research, 2013).

people to master if they are to be happy and successful in their lives. Our teachers design learning in two ways; they don't just think about subject content; they also design learning opportunities that encourage mastery of these skills, attitudes, dispositions and behaviours. Central to our pedagogy is the notion of choice. Currently youngsters are given choices about how they learn, where they learn and how they present their learning. As we develop, we will be offering choices about what youngsters learn and about the length of time they spend on their learning. By offering authentic choice, we have opened up the possibilities for collaboration in learning. We have become used to seeing youngsters learning in self-directed teams, with learning spilling out into our corridors and stairwells as youngsters take ownership and show real responsibility for their learning.

Honywood's approach to engaging parents is similarly thoughtful:

All research and advice tells us that there is no right way in which to parent. Each of us has a different family background and a unique set of personal circumstances which shape our parenting. Each child is also different: what will 'work' for one child may not 'work' for another.

A problem shared is a problem halved and having someone to talk to can prove invaluable.

We aim to establish an atmosphere in which situations and problems can be discussed in a confidential and supportive way, hopefully empowering you to be able to return home to your own individual situation armed with ideas and the knowledge that there are people out there, particularly the Family Learning Team and the Cohort Leaders at Honywood, who can support you.

We are happy to help you with a range of problems including:

- Supporting your child through friendship challenges.

- Communicating with my adolescent.

- My adolescent can't cope with exam stress, is there any help?

- Bereavement and loss.

- Internet safety.

- Who you can turn to when things get tough.

You'll remember that the CBI called for closer cooperation between schools and families, as one of their headline recommendations. Here it is in vibrant, successful action.

Scaling up

Each of these very different schools has in some real way demonstrated that it is possible to offer educational experiences that systematically develop confident and agile minds – and get great results. But a smattering of schools, you might argue, can hardly change the world. In addition to these living examples of the way forward we need ways of disseminating and scaling up what they are doing. And there are indeed tried and tested ways in which such good ideas can and do get magnified and broadcast. Here are a few.

One of the simplest is called a school cluster. Clusters were originally developed in the middle of the 20th century as a means of sharing resources across schools, especially in rural areas. Schools could share expensive resources – a swimming pool, a theatre or a specialist facility. But these days it's increasingly how schools are organising their own professional development too. (Maybe your school is part of a cluster, sometimes also called an academy chain.)

Under the Blair government, clusters of schools were actively encouraged by the National College[8] as a means of spreading ideas which might improve schools, and it is clear that they did have some success.[9] Most recently, borrowing the idea of the teaching hospital from the NHS, successful schools were invited to become 'teaching schools' with the responsibility of gathering clusters of schools around them to share good practice. Specifically they were given the opportunity to organise initial teacher training and organise professional development for teachers. By November 2013, there were 357 teaching schools and 301 teaching school alliances in England. The idea of such alliances is to encourage locally led self-improvement. Sounds like a good idea.

But if we tell you that a school can only be a teaching school if it is graded 'outstanding' by Ofsted, then you can immediately see a problem. For if the main criterion for admission is Ofsted's judgement, then the kinds of activities which such alliances promote may well be skewed towards

8 This body has been renamed twice in its short life in ways that clearly point to prevailing political opinions. First it was the National College for School Leadership, then the National College for Leadership of Schools and Children's Services. It became the National College for Teaching and Leadership in 2013.

9 See Alison Lock, *Clustering Together to Advance School Improvement: Working Together in Peer Support with an External Colleague* (Nottingham: National College for Leadership of Schools and Children's Services, 2000).

the kinds of activities which are approved of by Ofsted, but not the kinds which we have seen at Miriam Lord or North Shore. We know hundreds of schools which would make excellent teaching schools that would be graded merely 'good' by Ofsted. Their ethos might well be more conducive to real-world learning than those which happened to have got the 'outstanding' mark.

In some cases teaching schools have set out their stall with an agenda that is closer to ours than to Ofsted's. An example of this is St Ambrose Barlow Roman Catholic High School in Salford. Again there is a passionate and well-informed head teacher at work, Marie Garside. Over several years Marie has adopted her version of what she calls the creative curriculum – 'developing in all students the creativity to be able to thrive throughout their lifetimes'. Recently the teaching alliance she leads has become a hub for expansive education in the north-west. Marie and her cluster of schools have chosen to focus on teacher research. She believes that student outcomes are likely to improve if schools can engage with deep questions about the subjects they teach. The alliance is linked to the two universities in Manchester, which help them to explore science and engineering, as well as research methods, and also has long-standing relationships with cultural organisations such as galleries and museums across the region.

But the reason we mention them here is that we know that clusters of schools working together are great ways of growing and nurturing more innovation. We just need to ensure that the goal of any imaginary 'Mod School Alliance' is to create more opportunities of the kind that we have been describing in this book, and not merely to improve test scores in a range of academic subjects.

In a small way we have been involved in developing an extended cluster of like-minded schools under the banner of the Expansive Education Network. The hundreds of schools and thousands of teachers, many from overseas, that are part of this group explicitly choose to associate themselves with three of the core beliefs which have run throughout this book. First, they seek to *expand* the goals of education beyond traditional success criteria to include the kinds of habits of mind we talked about earlier. Second, they want to *expand* young people's capacity to deal with a lifetime of tricky things. Third, they want to *expand* their compass beyond the school gates. Expansive education assumes that rich learning challenges and opportunities abound in young people's out-of-school lives of music, sport, community and family activities.

At this point you may be wondering whatever happened to local educational authorities. Weren't they meant to be doing this kind of thing – supporting groups of local schools to get better? Indeed they were. But, sadly, too many of them became casualties of political warfare, were drained of financial support and shrivelled up, died out completely or became privatised. And some, truth to tell, weren't very good. But a few remain and are thriving. One is the East London borough of Thurrock, which is small enough to gather all of its head teachers together in a large room to really think things through and large enough to have some capability to support schools to develop. Thurrock is flying a flag for expansive education, with all of its schools being encouraged to experiment with new and innovative ways of teaching children, and all the while engaging teachers in evaluating this. (We know, by the way, from the work of researchers such as Professor John Hattie that when teachers become learners again their teaching improves, as does the achievement of their pupils.) Thurrock has decided that it can create a climate in which children can be taught to be creative and resilient at the same time as improving test results. To make sure that teachers and parents understand what they are up to, they have launched an annual awards ceremony to make this point.

The London Challenge is perhaps the best-known example of how clusters of schools can join forces to change the way they do things. Led by Sir Tim Brighouse, a highly experienced and inspirational local authority leader, it was conceived with a strong moral purpose: that every young person in London should receive a good or better education than they were receiving then (in 2003). The London Challenge had a powerful focus on leadership, teaching and learning, and pioneered the use of data (information about every aspect of children's learning and achievements) for the sole purpose of improvement not punishment. The idea of a clear challenge, coupled with a well-defined programme of action, will be apparent as we go through this chapter, and it is one that we return to in the last chapter of the book, as we believe it can be adapted for our purposes as a call to action.

Employers

If the necessary changes are going to happen, though, there is a strong need for support – and pressure – from outside the education system as well as within it. We mentioned the main employers' organisation, the CBI, and their publication, *First Steps: A New Approach For Our Schools*, in Chapter 1. As well as saying the kinds of things which we might expect an employers' organisation to say – for instance, bemoaning the low levels of literacy and numeracy of English school-leavers compared with many other countries – *First Steps* laid out a different set of demands, prefaced by this powerful statement:

Change is possible – but we must be clearer about what we ask schools to develop in students and for what purpose.

You could imagine, just for a moment, that employers had been secretly studying the kinds of books and papers we have been reading (and writing) over the last two decades. But they may perfectly well have come to the same conclusions by themselves. Here are three of the things they called for:

1. The development of a clear, widely owned and stable statement of the outcomes that all schools are asked to deliver. This should go beyond the merely academic, into the behaviours and attitudes schools should foster in everything they do. It should be the basis on which we judge all new policy ideas, schools and the structures that society sets up to monitor them.

2. The adoption by schools of a strategy for fostering parental engagement and wider community involvement, including links with business.

3. The Department for Education should accelerate its programme of decentralisation of control for all schools in England. This should be extended to schools in other parts of the UK, freeing head teachers to deliver real improvements.

First Steps is really a manifesto for a radical change to the way we currently organise schooling. Its central demands chime strongly with our own long-held views. The first of their suggestions – that we should go beyond the subjects on the curriculum to think more profoundly about what it is we think the outcomes of schooling should be – aligns most strongly with the agenda we have laid out. Their second recommendation – that we should empower parents to engage with schools – is the focus of the next chapter.

In our research for this book we have spoken with hundreds of parents, students, teachers and head teachers. In the course of our conversations, we were struck by the letter below as an example of exactly the kind of thing the CBI is calling for.

Letter from a parent to her child's primary head teacher

Dear Head Teacher,

I want to write and thank you for recently running the parent workshops on how to support our children in 'Building Learning Power'. Your talk has given me a vocabulary to use when talking to my children to help convey some truly important values that I have always believed to be vital to both success and happiness. Specifically that 'effort is more important than ability' and 'mistakes are part of the learning process/to succeed you have to be prepared to take the risk of failing'. I loved the analogy you used of the brain being a muscle that has to be exercised and made fit for learning. I have been talking a lot about overcoming adversity with my children.

As you know, we are lucky enough to have a talented child in your school, but her aversion to challenges and her sometimes rather thin skin regarding mistakes have worried us. However, after the workshops we now feel more resourceful in dealing with her reticence *and* we have the start of a language that we can use to help her. We have seen an immediate impact on her from the school's initiative to build a positive attitude to learning; we have seen our daughter fight back her immediate inclination to want to give up on things when they become tricky and we have praised her for it.

We realise it is still early days and we will have to work hard not to fall back into old bad habits of rescuing and reassuring her! Well done though; you have opened the debate, set us a challenge and given us some very useful tools, ideas and initiatives to go forward with as a family. Thank you for a very important beginning.

All the best,

Teresa, Year 4 mum

At the end of 2014 the CBI published an 'end of year report' on their *First Steps* agenda. On every aspect they rated the government poorly using marks that ranged between B- to D! The D went for the first of their suggestions, that we develop a clear statement of the outcomes that all schools should deliver:

The eco-system of a school should foster academic success, but also go beyond it to the development of the

behaviours and attitudes that really set young people up
for adult life.[10]

In language which even more strongly echoes our own, they
go on to specify these behaviours and attitudes:

Characteristics, values and habits that last a lifetime	
The system should encourage people to be	*This means helping to instil the following attributes*
Determined	Grit, resilience, tenacity
	Self-control
	Curiosity
Optimistic	Enthusiasm and zest
	Gratitude
	Confidence and ambition
	Creativity
Emotionally intelligent	Humility
	Respect and good manners
	Sensitivity to global concerns

The message is obvious. Many employers have a clear vision
of what the desired outcomes of school should be for young
people, but so far the government is not listening. Hence the

10 CBI, *First Steps: A New Approach For Our Schools. End of Year Report* (London:
CBI, 2013). Available at: http://www.cbi.org.uk/media/2473815/
First_steps_end_of_year_report.pdf.

D grade awarded to the Department for Education. But the pressure will mount. Employers in the UK are a powerful group, not to be idly dismissed by governments. They are helping to create a climate in which our balanced approach can and will flourish.

Professional bodies

Two teacher bodies are currently asking and answering the kinds of questions which we have been posing. In the UK, the Association of School and College Leaders and its 'Great Education Debate' have stimulated useful thinking. The debate takes as its starting point this statement:

> We believe that it is time for everyone with a stake in education to have a say about the future of our schools and colleges policy – employers, parents, young people, academics, politicians, teachers, school and college leaders. We want to create a vision and a plan that everyone can sign up to.[11]

The Great Education Debate recently published a summary of its conclusions.[12] These centre on the idea of a school-led, self-improving system. Now, this may sound like jargon to some readers, but read on a little more in this document and you will find many recommendations that mirror those we

11 See www.greateducationdebate.org.uk/.
12 ASCL, *Leading for the Future: A Summation of the Great Education Debate* (London: ASCL, 2014). Available at: http://view.vcab. com/?vcabid=geaSeneagSclphnln.

have been suggesting. Here is a flavour, some echoing the CBI suggestions we have been exploring:

In an ideal world we would debate these issues and reach a shared view on the purpose of education. We would determine the relative weight to be accorded to the differing drivers. That would then inform the framing and the content of the curriculum ... This is not as far-fetched as it sounds: other countries such as Singapore do precisely this.

We need to facilitate systematically the professional development and lifelong learning of existing teachers.

Any definition of the purpose of education would surely include maximising the life chances of all young people by making them work-ready, life-ready and ready for further learning.

The unique challenges of the world in the 21st century require a better understanding of the underpinning personal capacities that are the difference between the success and failure of otherwise identical young people.[13]

The last of these opinions speaks poignantly to the comments of many of the young people we have quoted in the book.

A second initiative called 'Redesigning Schooling' has been stimulated by a professional body called The Schools

---

13 ASCL, *Leading for the Future*.

Network.[14] At the heart of Redesigning Schooling is a plea for the teaching profession, especially school principals, to take charge of the debate about the future of education. They say:

These are tough times for school leaders but we know as a profession we have to change. Surely we have to have the courage of our convictions and put in place those opportunities that we feel equip our students most appropriately for life in the digital age and for taking their place in the global workspace?

Do we always have to follow the Government line, or can we as a profession take more control of the future of education and the steering of our young people towards global citizenship? Redesigning Schooling is a campaign lead by SSAT and its member schools, leading thinkers and academics to shape the teaching profession's own vision for schooling.[15]

Precisely because it is seeking to develop debate and innovation within the teaching profession itself, Redesigning Schooling is necessarily taking time to build its point of view. But, through its events and publications, it is encouraging school leaders to articulate with greater confidence their

14 We have contributed two pamphlets to the Redesigning Schooling campaign: Guy Claxton and Bill Lucas, *What Kind of Teaching for What Kind of Learning?* (London, SSAT, 2013). Available at: http://www.ssatuk.co.uk/wp-content/uploads/2013/09/Claxton-and-Lucas-What-kind-of-teaching-chapter-1.pdf; and Bill Lucas, *Engaging Parents: Why and How* (London, SSAT, 2013). Available at: http://www.ssatuk.co.uk/wp-content/uploads/2013/09/RS6-Engaging-parents-why-and-how-chapter-one.pdf.

15 See http://www.redesigningschooling.org.uk/campaign/campaign-hopes/.

own vision of education. In the next chapter we will look at ways in which we can all accelerate the changes we want to see.

We've also referred to the Organisation for Economic Cooperation and Development (see Chapter 2). The OECD is the organisation which runs the Programme for International Student Assessment, home of the infamous PISA tests which all education ministries are keen to do so well on. (How educators love their acronyms!) The man who runs PISA is a German statistician called Andreas Schleicher. Many countries (including the UK) have become so mesmerised by the international league tables to which the PISA data gives rise that they can think of nothing more inspiring, as a goal for education, than to beat Finland or Shanghai in these tables. Many have argued that the very existence of these tables has driven education systems around the world in a regressive direction. Some countries – Wales is cited as being one – have even started to tailor their education systems specifically to improve their PISA rankings.[16] It's not that it's a bad idea for countries to know how they are doing in teaching maths, English and science; it's just that, if these paper and pencil tests are given undue weight, they start to eclipse other good educational goals – like the habits of mind – that can't be so easily measured.

Schleicher himself is all too aware of this danger. In fact, his own model of education is a well-balanced one (see the figure opposite). It is easy to see how the things we have been arguing for in Chapters 1–4 can be fitted into his four rectangles. He is trying to broaden out the PISA tests so they do actually assess things like students' capacity for collaborative

---

16 See William Stewart, How PISA came to rule the world, *TES* (6 December 2013). Available at: http://www.tes.co.uk/article. aspx?storycode=6379225.

problem-solving or creativity. This is not easy to do, but the OECD is leading the research in this area.[17]

Dimensions and challenges for a 21st century curriculum

Knowledge	Skills
Balance conceptual and practical and connect the content to real-world relevance	Developing higher-order skills such as the 4Cs: creativity, critical thinking, communication, collaboration
Character	**Meta-layer**
Nurturing behaviours and values for a changing and challenging world: adaptability, persistence, resilience and moral-related traits (integrity, justice, empathy)	Learning how to learn, interdisciplinary, systems thinking

Source: Andreas Schleicher (ed.), *Preparing Teachers and Developing School Leaders for the 21st Century: Lessons from around the World* (Paris: OECD Publishing, 2012).

Two examination boards have also been actively seeking to broaden what it is that schools do; they are City & Guilds and Pearson. City & Guilds have been promoting research into the practical learning and apprenticeships which so

---

17 See, for example, OECD, *PISA 2015: Draft Collaborative Problem Solving Framework* (March 2013). Available at: http://www.oecd.org/callsfortenders/Annex%20ID_PISA%202015%20Collaborative%20Problem%20Solving%20Framework%20.pdf.

many young people want, in order to help schools and colleges provide more effectively for the many students who do not choose an academic route. As contributors to this research, we have been vocal in suggesting that, as with schools more generally, we need to think about what else, other than routine skills, young people should be learning. In particular, we have suggested that they need to learn to be resourceful (able to deal with the non-routine), to develop pride in their work (thinking like a craftsman, never accepting the slapdash and always striving to do their very best) and build a set of wider skills beyond the particular vocational pathway on which they are embarked.[18]

Pearson has contributed to the debate by commissioning research into young people's views of school.[19] The central conclusion of this study was that it was "difficult for them to understand the relevance of school learning to their future work aims".

There appeared to be three causes of this disconnection:

1. Little association between lesson content and career preferences.

2. Teachers not knowing their pupils' hopes and dreams.

3. Inadequate opportunities to gain foundation 'life skills'.

Students also express the need for learning that relates to their goals. They are hungry for that connection, and speak

---

18 See Bill Lucas, Ellen Spencer and Guy Claxton, *How to Teach Vocational Education: A Theory of Vocational Pedagogy* (London: City & Guilds Centre for Skills Development, 2012). Available at: http://www.skillsdevelopment.org/PDF/How-to-teach-vocational-education.pdf.

19 See http://uk.pearson.com/myeducation/my-education-report.html.

easily and specifically about what they want to do with their lives.

Here are some of the points the student interviewees made:

Once we leave school we'll need to be much more independent, so we should learn things that will help us later on.

Teachers shouldn't just be at the front – they should interact in the classroom.

Schools need to let us know more about the future, jobs and help us to know more about careers, relating learning and work ...

I have never been asked about my hopes and dreams.

Teachers could make their classes more relevant to my future goals by asking what I wanted to do in the future and help me try to achieve those targets by helping me in the areas I need help in.

Whatever these students' schools, backgrounds and ambitions, their voice is not one of hostile disaffection. They are thoughtful and articulate, and the points they make are important and thought-provoking. If the groundswell for change is to gather momentum, students themselves will be powerful participants in the process.

The third sector

Finally in this chapter we shouldn't forget the role that is being played by charitable bodies. Of course, some of them are quite capable of campaigning for versions of education which are narrow and backwards-looking. But most are motivated by big moral ideas – social justice, increased well-being, cohesion, better care of our planet and lifelong learning. Some undertake research. Others produce resources. Some are funding bodies. Others lobby for the changes they desire. Although it is somewhat invidious to mention just a few examples, nevertheless we are going to do just that!

The Royal Society for the Encouragement of Arts, Manufactures and Commerce (or the RSA as it is more widely known) has a long history of educational innovation. In 1980 it published a manifesto called *Education for Capability* which made many of the same points we are highlighting in this book.[20] More than a decade ago, the RSA suggested that we could organise what teachers teach not into subjects but into 'themes' and 'competencies'. They called it Opening Minds.[21] Some 200 schools have now adopted its principles.

When Opening Minds was first introduced most schools organised what they taught according to subjects. So your child might have a lesson of English, then one of geography or science and so on. Look at a typical secondary school timetable and, odds-on, it will still be organised in this way, with five or six different subjects in roughly hour-long blocks each day. The RSA turned this on its head and asked a

---

20 RSA, *Education for Capability Manifesto* (London: RSA, 1980).
21 See www.rsaopeningminds.org.uk/.

148

different question. What would school look like if we organised it in terms of the competences we wanted students to develop rather than by subject area? They came up with five such competences: citizenship, learning, managing information, relating to people and managing situations. These kinds of things are much closer to what we called utilities in Chapter 4. Here's an example of what they thought might go into managing situations:

- Time management – students understand the importance of managing their own time, and develop preferred techniques for doing so.

- Coping with change – students understand what is meant by managing change, and develop a range of techniques for use in varying situations.

- Feelings and reactions – students understand the importance of both celebrating success and managing disappointment, and ways of handling these.

- Creative thinking – students understand what is meant by being entrepreneurial and initiative-taking, and how to develop their capacities in these areas.

- Risk-taking – students understand how to manage risk and uncertainty, including the wide range of contexts in which these will be encountered and techniques for managing them.

You could theoretically just replace subjects with competences and end up designing a curriculum of one-hour blocks looking at time management or risk-taking. But such an approach would clearly be (a) silly and (b) entirely against the spirit of what Opening Minds is proposing. These competences need to be developed through rigorous projects and enquiries of the kind that we were suggesting would feature in a Key Stage 3 curriculum.

Think of one of your pupils (if you are a teacher) or your children (if you are a parent) and the situations they encounter, or think about yourself and the kinds of things you need to manage in your own life. Whether it's the weekly shop, homework, getting ready for a holiday or football practice, we all need to be able to manage time. Similarly, in a fast-moving world, we all need to be able to deal with change. Do we embrace it? Do we get grumpy and resist it? Do we ask for help? Do we find out more? Do we think of different ways in which we could react and select the most appropriate one? We think it is clear that these examples of managing situations are manifestly things that help life go more smoothly and effectively and, therefore, qualities you'd want the next generation to have.

This highlighting of useful habits of mind, and weaving them more systematically into lessons, is no great revolution. Both New Zealand and Australia, for example, have chosen to organise their schools by foregrounding the capabilities they want students to acquire in the course of studying important things. You cannot teach competences in isolation; they have to have content too. Opening Minds schools tend to assume that the organisation of the school day may, in part at least, be about creating chunks of time where pupils can work with teachers, employers and others on rigorous, challenging enquiries or projects. By doing this, pupils learn 'how to' at the same time as they think about the whys and whats of any discipline.

Here's one more example of a charitable body creating optimism on the ground. The Sutton Trust describes itself as a 'do tank' (as opposed to a 'think tank'). We think it has a place in this chapter because of its close links to the real world of schools. It is trying explicitly to use research to change policy and practice. Above all, the Sutton Trust is trying to help children who are less well-off do better at school and then in life – what's often referred to as improving social mobility.

A practical example of what they produce, in collaboration with the Education Endowment Foundation (EEF), is the Teaching and Learning Toolkit for teachers.[22] The toolkit takes a number of different teaching methods and then distils the research on its effectiveness into a really clear 'dashboard' that signals its degree of impact, cost to implement, the strength of the evidence in its favour (the icon that looks like a weight or possibly a fashionable handbag!) and then gives it an overall score in terms of the number of months by which it might accelerate pupils' progress. Not all the teaching methods they have evaluated are directed at building up students' habits of mind – some are only assessed in terms of their effect on traditional examination grades – but some of them are.

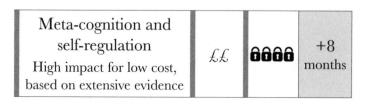

For example, the screen grab above shows the dashboard for teaching strategies that develop metacognition and self-regulation – two of the most powerful habits of mind we have been focusing on. Strategies for building metacognition

---

22 See www.suttontrust.com/about-us/education-endowment-foundation/ teaching-learning-toolkit/.

involve getting the students to think more explicitly about their own learning. For example, they are asked to set goals, anticipate how much time a task will take, evaluate their own work or step back and check the way they have been working or discussing to see if they can improve their modus operandi. (We looked at some of the strategies for building self-regulation in Chapter 3.) For example, they might include learning how to manage distractions or how to use motivational self-talk in the way that athletes and sportspeople regularly do. The evidence for the effectiveness of these strategies is strong, especially (but not entirely) with children who have been making slower progress. Overall, adopting these kinds of strategies in the classroom accelerates students' progress by as much as eight months. And the costs are relatively low, mainly relating to professional development that shows teachers how these strategies are best implemented. If teachers can help students to get better test scores, and at the same time give them mental habits that are useful in all kinds of real-life situations, how could anyone possibly object?

To sum up: the future of schools, as we suggested at the start of this chapter, is already here, even if it is not yet equally available to all of our children. In the next chapter we offer a few suggestions of things that can be done by parents at home and then, in the final chapter, invite you to consider taking action on a broader stage.

Chapter 6

What parents can do at home

I've been making a list of the things they don't teach you at school. They don't teach you how to love somebody. They don't teach you how to be famous. They don't teach you how to be rich or how to be poor. They don't teach you how to walk away from someone you don't love any longer. They don't teach you how to know what's going on in someone else's mind. They don't teach you what to say to someone who's dying. They don't teach you anything worth knowing.

Neil Gaiman, *The Sandman:*
***The Kindly Ones*, Vol. 9**

Preparing young people to thrive in a tricky world is not just the job of schools and teachers. Parents are educators too. The way we talk to our kids, the kinds of rituals we create for them around mealtimes and bedtimes, the activities we encourage, the role models we provide, the materials we place within their reach, the kinds of 'fun' we lay on for them: all of these carry messages that influence their growing minds – for good or ill. Before we try to think about how we can help to shape the education system itself – what we can all do to encourage the spread of the kinds of schools that our kids really need – we need to look closer to home (literally). What is the informal 'domestic curriculum' we are providing for our children, and could we do a tiny bit better?

We should say, of course, that, just as the earlier chapters were written for the purposes of stimulating debate, so this chapter on home learning is meant to do likewise. There are hundreds of excellent books on parenting and parental engagement in children's learning and we certainly do not intend to duplicate them here.[1] Instead, we offer this as a starter-for-ten to get parents and teachers thinking about the 'how' of learning at home. Remember Ruby and her seven Cs? We will use her description of the attributes she values as a way of organising our discussion. Naturally, you may not like our seven Cs and might prefer to come up with your own. We'd love you to do that!

The domestic curriculum, as we have implied, is like the one children learn at school; but it is conveyed more by the way things are done than the specific 'lessons' we might try to teach. You can play a family game of Scrabble, for example, in a way that models your total engagement in a good game; or as a coach, less interested in winning and more in making suggestions to your children as to how they can

---

1 Bill has written a couple of these – see Bill Lucas and Stephen Briers, *Happy Families: How to Make One, How to Keep One* (Harlow: BBC Active, 2006); Bill Lucas and Alistair Smith, *Help Your Child to Succeed: The Essential Guide for Parents*, 2nd rev. edn (London: Network Continuum Education, 2009).

make good words, with all your letters visible to all so that everyone can think through their options out loud; or as a fiercely competitive test of your own verbal ability; or as an exercise in dutiful, half-hearted involvement with your family while you quietly check emails on your phone. It's not what you do, it's the way that you do it!

Confidence

Being confident involves developing and using a growth mindset, being a can-do person and being able to act independently. A growth mindset, as we saw in Chapter 2, is founded on self-belief. Children who believe they can get better at things, it turns out, normally can – with practice and determination. The fixed mindset makes you fatalistic, so you don't think it is worth doing the very things – practising and struggling – that could help you to improve. The best ways in which you can encourage your child to develop this kind of self-belief is to avoid too much generalised praise (Well done, Guy) or 'ability' praise (Guy, you're just a natural at this), and concentrate instead on giving really specific feedback to your child when he does things well (I really liked the way you spent extra time on your homework, Guy, and used the ideas your teacher had given you for writing interesting sentences). Guy, in this final example, is hearing that his effort paid off and, over time, he will see how valuable it is to go the extra mile. Another important job for parents and family members is to share things with which they are struggling. In this way, children learn that struggling and making mistakes are normal and healthy aspects of learning.

You can't give a child a magic injection of confidence! For sure, you can make them feel loved and secure, but real inner can-do confidence comes from the experiences of planning and seeing difficult tasks through. A key part of such success involves the ability to set goals and then plan how you will achieve them. So, from an early age it is helpful if you can get into the habit of making plans as a family (What shall we do while we are on holiday? Who'd like to suggest what we do today?). Once children are at school, homework (not always a helpful activity if poorly set) provides a good opportunity to help your child break a task down into its smaller components, think through how long each part might take, make a plan, do it and then, whenever possible, talk about how it went.

When they are very young children want and need you to hold their hand. But as they grow you can help them to practise acting independently. To begin with you can be quietly there in the background – for example, while they cook a simple meal 'on their own'. Then you can set them simple jobs to accomplish as they grow in confidence – walking the short distance to a local shop and buying you something, taking the dog for a walk (with you seeing them safely over the main road first), getting everything ready for school the night before.

A good read to help you understand more about developing confidence is Carol Dweck's *Mindset*.

Curiosity

Curiosity is at the heart of all learning. Being curious involves noticing things, reading avidly and, obviously, asking good questions. Young children have curiosity in great abundance, constantly pestering those around them with questions (Where does dew come from? Why does it get dark? Who is God?). But it is all too easy to dampen children's insatiable appetite to find out more. It can be wearying to answer yet another question, but if you can possibly manage to show genuine interest in the enquiry, such role modelling will be a powerful influence.

Being able to notice things is an essential component of curiosity. For some children (and adults) it seems to come naturally. For others it may need to be actively coaxed into life. If you have ever been to an art gallery you will have an idea of what we mean. Some visitors seem to be able to see things in pictures that others completely miss. It's the same with children. On a walk to school, for example, some children chatter away naming things as they go. Others talk less but you can tell that they are noticing for they tell you about it later. A third category of child (and adult!) seems to walk through life without obviously noticing what is new or different or interesting. Parents and family members can help by playing games (the obvious one is I-Spy) and explicitly talking out loud as they go about any daily tasks. It can feel very odd, but it helps (Can you see the ...? Isn't it interesting the way that ...? What do think that is?). Family walks and car journeys are great ways of practising noticing. And with a smartphone in your hand children can be motivated by taking photos which they can return to later and discuss.

Reading for pleasure is probably the most important habit you can instil in your child. Some children take to it and need little encouragement, just a ready supply of books from the library. Others need lots of patient encouragement. There is nothing more powerful than a whole family reading their books together. Children see their parents engrossed in a book and inwardly record the importance attached to the activity by the grown-ups. Routines help – for example, making uninterrupted time after lunch at weekends and in the holidays can work. Before they go to sleep is a good time to take the opportunity to practise reading together. If your child is reluctant then you will need all your skill to find topics of interest. One neat way of persuading reluctant children to read is to give them the chance to turn off their light really late occasionally at a weekend *only* if they are reading a book. Reading aloud to your children for as long as they will let you is vital. It helps if you can have lots of children's books at a low height throughout your home.

Questions are the outward expression of our curiosity, and the home is the obvious place to give them full rein. Simple things that work include: watching a wildlife programme together and then talking about it; making sure you have a good supply of simple reference books around the place – dictionaries, atlases, guidebooks and so on; getting your children to create a treasure hunt around your house/garden and make up the clues; sitting beside your child and doing an internet search for something that one of you is curious about.

A good resource for encouraging curiosity is the BBC iWonder website or the Discovery Channel, and a wonderful book is Michael Rosen's *Good Ideas*.[2]

Conviviality and collaboration

Conviviality and collaboration are core attributes of human beings. Conviviality is close to what Malcolm Gladwell helpfully calls 'social savvy', and it seems that the home is a really good place to develop it. Young children can be very sensitive about who their friends are, worrying that they are in the wrong crowd or that someone does not like them. In the home we can provide children with a safe environment to practise interacting with people of all ages. We can show them how we are all individual and different and how to value such differences. Whether it's being part of a tribe, group, team or family, we need to be able to get on with people, even those we don't like very much. Spotting an acquaintance across a room at a party, Abraham Lincoln famously remarked, "I don't like that man. I must get to know him better." That's a good attitude to model to our children. Whether on Facebook or in the playground, children cannot help encountering hostility, prejudice and the rush to judge. Being convivial – a good collaborator – requires us to be able to listen empathically, show kindness to others and give and receive feedback well.

Empathy is the capacity of seeing the world from someone else's perspective. For a parent, learning to listen to your child with empathy is one of the hardest things to do. It is all

---

2 Michael Rosen, *Good Ideas: How To Be Your Child's (and Your Own) Best Teacher* (London: John Murray, 2014).

too easy either to jump in and give advice or to cut short a child's distressed explanation because we want to reassure him or her. Much of what empathic listeners do is non-verbal. Short noises like 'uh-huh', 'mmm', 'ahh', with small nods of the head and an absolute focus on what the speaker is saying are important. A useful technique widely used in counselling is to try to paraphrase what you think you have heard and offer it back to your child: "So, it sounds like you're pretty unhappy about …", "I'm wondering if you might be feeling …" or "It sounds like you are thinking about …" With some careful listening you can keep narrowing the focus of your paraphrasing until you are pretty confident you have caught the nub of what they are saying. There are various games and activities that you can use to develop your child's empathy. Examples include pinning names of famous characters on the back of a child with them having to guess who it is, games like What's My Line? and role play between different real and imaginary people.

You can't teach kindness. That's a bold statement, but we believe it to be true in the sense that there is no simple training activity you can employ. Rather, it requires careful choice of language to select adjectives that are more generous than they are critical ("She must be going through a really tough time" rather than "Isn't Aunty Helen being really cranky?"). As well as modelling it also invites us to correct our children by offering kinder versions of critical statements they may make, as well as looking for examples from your family or in the news of kind behaviour on which you can provide a commentary. And, of course, actions speak louder than words. The way you treat your partner/ spouse, as well as your wider family and friends, will be a strong influence on your children. Some homes give reward systems, for example for chores. It is also possible to use the same system for acts of kindness.

Being convivial does not mean that you can never criticise others. On the contrary, as we have suggested, feedback is one of the most effective means by which we learn and grow. Rather, it's a question of how you give and receive critical comments. In terms of giving it is helpful to find positive things to notice first, to focus on one or two specific things and to be sure that you suggest a way of doing things differently. When it comes to suggesting different courses of action a phrase we like is: "You might like to …" In terms of receiving feedback the most important gift you can give your child is not to act defensively. By means of both body language and words, show them how important it is just to listen and learn. That's not to say that all feedback is accurate! You can help your child accept what she hears but also have the inner confidence to be critical of her actions in a different way from the feedback giver. Giving and receiving feedback has to be practised so that individuals find the words and body language which are most suited to them and therefore have the ring of authenticity.

A good book to read is *Raising Caring, Capable Kids with Habits of Mind* by Lauren Carner and Angela Ladavaia-Cox.[3]

---

3 Lauren Carner and Angela Ladavaia-Cox, *Raising Caring, Capable Kids with Habits of Mind* (Mechanicsburg, PA: Institute for Habits of Mind, 2012).

Communication

Being communicative is very important. So much unhappiness stems from accidental misunderstandings or careless explanations. Top of many parents' worry list is a perception that either their children can't communicate with them or they can't get through to their children. Teenagers have got a bad name (with some justification!) for the grunts and mumbling which they may offer their parents in response to questions. Sometimes this is partly the result of what parents do – for example, the parent who pounces on their child freshly home from school to demand what they did at school (a sure turn-off, sadly). Sometimes it is a deliberate tactic of children to keep their parents in blissful ignorance of their misdemeanours. "Yeah, whatever" is a current favourite push-back, but by the time you read this there will be new variants! It turns out that being able to communicate well with your children, especially during adolescence, is a strong influence on their performance at school.

At the most personal level, being able to name and talk about feelings is fundamentally important. There is no short cut to finding opportunities for your child to experience and then give a name to the full range of feelings. Without this they cannot express themselves effectively. In the early years the Roger Hargreaves characters are wonderful (Mr Happy, Mr Grumpy, etc.). Then you can speculate on what others might be feeling in stories, in the news and in your own family. Always you are trying to create a climate in which children feel able to express their feelings and be listened to as they do so. A harder and equally important lesson for children is the realisation that no one can make them feel something. Even if they are angry or sad, they have choices.

They can lash out or be quiet or plan to do something different. Once children can recognise and name their feelings they are well on the way to recognising their own trigger points and 'sore spots', which tend to cause them to react in ways which are less helpful, and start to find better ways of dealing with them.

Communication is not a context-free zone! It involves learning how to offer opinions. Some children seem to find this easy (for them, *not* always offering their opinion is the challenge). Most children have opinions but do not always know how or when to share them. Around the kitchen table is the perfect location for children to practise. Or it can be done as a game: for example, playing Just a Minute (or Just a Half Minute if 60 seconds seems too long at first). At some point your child will be asked to prepare a speech or presentation at school, and it will be all the harder for them if they haven't practised already in the safety of the home.

While the kitchen, bedroom, classroom and playground may be the main early environments for children, there are many other situations in which they will need to learn to match their language to their audience. This can easily be rehearsed, simulated and practised at home using role play and games. At the simplest level, when your child has a tricky situation (e.g. feeling they have been unfairly treated by a teacher or by a friend) you can get them to rehearse with you different ways in which they might have a conversation. You can show them how, through their choice of different forms of words, they may get very different responses. You can have lots of fun with this!

A really practically helpful book is *Stick Up for Yourself* by Gershen Kaufman.[4]

Creativity

Being creative is one of the ways in which your child will be able to distinguish himself or herself from their peers. It involves having good ideas, dealing with uncertainty and being able to make links between apparently unconnected things. A number of well-respected thinkers about education believe that creativity is being squeezed out of some schools because of an obsession with tests and exams (and we are inclined to agree).

Having a good idea when you need one is central to creativity, but it is not much taught in schools. All too often children are asked to write a story or paint a picture without the process of creativity itself being explored. We know, for example, that human beings are not good at having ideas if they are under stress. (Evolutionarily we are programmed to fight or flight, and not to debate or mull when we are under attack.) So children need to be given lots of practice time to have new ideas when they are feeling most relaxed – after a game, after listening to music, when they are being cuddled by us. We can also give them various tools and let them experiment. Into this category come brainstorming, using a mind map, making a list, closing your eyes and picturing and so on. Some children like to keep an ideas book/folder/file, either hard copy or on a tablet. The big barrier with creativity for most children/people is the fear of making mistakes

---

4 Gershen Kaufman, *Stick Up for Yourself: Every Kid's Guide to Personal Power and Self-Esteem* (Minneapolis, MN: Free Spirit Publishing, 1999).

or getting it wrong, and you will want to do all you can to help them learn how to 'park' this side of their brain sometimes.

Uncertainty is an inevitable part of life, and it demands creativity. If everything were straightforward and predictable, with no ifs and buts, then we would not need to be creative and think differently. Creativity isn't just for filling up idle time by painting a picture! Being able to manage uncertainty creatively calls for resilience as well. It requires us to explore and tolerate feelings of, for example, confusion or inadequacy. Hopefully we will get set many problems at school to which there is no easy answer. We will have to wrestle with degrees of likelihood. Games of chance and risk are good ways of trying out these kinds of issues at home. Or you might like to take a tricky item of news for an older child and explore possible courses of action. These kinds of activities can be grouped together under the banner of 'What if' – what would you do if you found yourself in a position where …?

Making connections and seeing patterns is an important part of being creative. Every time we use a metaphor we link one thing with another. Creative people have made great discoveries through the process of seeing connections where others have not. For example, someone thought to stitch together the invention of steam engines, the development of steel and the growing need for travel between the north and south of the UK, and generate the seed of an idea that became the railways. Mind maps are a good way of seeing connections, as are many other graphic depictions of ideas such as concept maps. Free association games can encourage connected thinking. The game of Crazy Connections (where you try and connect two highly unlikely items together) can be fun over a meal.

An excellent resource is *The Bright Stuff* by C. J. Simister or you could try one of ours, *The Creative Thinking Plan* (aimed more at adults but with ideas that are transferable).[5]

Commitment

Commitment to learning is essential if your children are going to find their passion in life. For children to find their passion – the things that really turn them on – parents and grandparents need to give them every opportunity to try things out. If you went to university, the metaphor you might like to have here is of home life as an extended freshers' fair, or think of a farmers' market. We need to create lots of opportunities for tasters. Some children find their passion easily. A special teacher ignites their interest. A talented family member takes them to the ice rink and they decide to learn ice hockey. But for most of us it is a slower, more uncertain process. The trick here is to gradually narrow the frame and set mutually agreed goals with your children about how long they might stick at something before they decide it's not for them. It's a difficult thing to judge. Bill, for example, knows that if he had not been forced through the early painful days of practising the French horn he would not have ended up enjoying playing it. A really simple thing to do with young children on wet holiday or weekend days is to refuse to answer their complaints that they are bored

---

5 C. J. Simister, *The Bright Stuff: Playful Ways to Nurture Your Child's Extraordinary Mind* (Harlow: Pearson Education, 2009); Guy Claxton and Bill Lucas, *The Creative Thinking Plan: How to Generate Ideas and Solve Problems in Your Work and Life* (London: BBC Books, 2004).

and equip them with a supply of cardboard boxes, scissors, sticky tape and their imagination, and see what happens.

Home life is full of opportunities for children to learn taking responsibility. Keeping pets is a good example of this. So too are the many chores that you can share out. A child can be shopper, cook, gardener, map-reader, budget-holder, event-planner and so forth. Sometimes the trick is just to make it sound a bit grown-up (rather than a childish task) to enlist their imaginative engagement.

Sticking with difficulty – being persistent – is eminently learnable and coachable too. The Building Learning Power approach has a simple idea, the 'stuck poster', for teachers to develop with children in their classrooms. Children pool ideas as to what they can do when they are stuck and don't know how to proceed, and they make a personal or class poster of these ideas as an aide-memoire. Art Costa and Bena Kallick's Habits of Mind programme[6] has a similar idea – the persistence toolbox. Either of these readily adapt themselves to the home. Think of homework time when your child is stuck and create a family version of this which your child could stick on the wall in their bedroom or maybe you could add it to the fridge door in the kitchen.

Craftsmanship

Sometimes we hear that being craftsmanlike is going out of fashion. In a 24/7 throwaway society it is all too easy to condone the slapdash. Being craftsmanlike requires us to show pride, learn from our mistakes, work on practising the hard bits and make something the best it can be.

---

6 See www.habitsofmind.co.uk/.

Most of us are naturally proud of something when we know we have done a good job. Unfortunately, in some schools, it has become uncool to show pride in your achievements. This is a terrible thing and we have to fix it. First base is to be clear that showing pride is a feature of your child's earliest memories. One ready way of recognising pride might be to create a family motto that somehow says, in a sentence, what your family is good at. Or you could go one stage further and create your own coat of arms (much fun as a family holiday activity!). Or how about creating an actual or virtual gallery of all the accomplished people in your family? Just the process of identifying who is good at what, or which of your ancestors was famous for something, can be very stimulating and enlightening.

We can all learn from our mistakes. Indeed, it is particularly helpful if this is regularly demonstrated by the whole family. Without suggesting for a moment that your conversations should be strewn with disasters and near-misses, it is really helpful when adults show that they too make mistakes; that making mistakes is normal and that the important thing is to bounce back and have a better go. Some children are fearful of blotting their page and of having to cross things out. A useful activity for a family is to look at a play, a painting, a building or an invention for which there are many prototypes or drafts and explore them together. That way it is crystal clear that making mistakes is another way of saying 'work in progress' and that most really good work goes through many versions. One person's version is another's mistake. Another fun thing to do as a family is to have a 'mistake of the week' award when different family members share gaffes or errors. Encourage them to say what they might do differently next time!

Practising and working on the hard bits is an essential feature of craftsmanship. If you are really going to be great at what you do, you have to be willing to do the grunt work as well as have fun. As an adult, stop and think about how you practise something that really matters to you – for example, if you have to give a speech at a wedding. Things that good practisers find useful include:

- Speeding it up.
- Slowing it down.
- Chunking a big task into lots of small ones.
- Doing it against the clock.
- Doing it blindfold.
- Doing it with notes.
- Doing it without notes.
- Getting feedback.
- Recording/filming and watching what you did.
- Doing the difficult things again and again.

Whether it is sport or music or irregular verbs or organising a school bag the night before, children need to practise, and you can help them by being a good role model and creating lots of opportunities for them.

If you want inspiration on craftmanship, google 'Austin's Butterfly' and marvel at how small children can be turned into little crafts people and draw better and better butterflies.[7] Children know only too well that mastery is born of effort, patience and a tolerance for frustration. It is only in

---

7   See www.youtube.com/watch?v=PZo2PIhnmNY.

school that you are told that you are 'gifted and talented' if you get things right, quickly, first time, always.

By trying things out in your own home it is much easier to appreciate the reality of what we have been discussing. Preparing children to face a lifetime of tricky stuff is, of course, tricky. But it is perfectly possible – you may remember the letter from Teresa, the mum who had been helped by her daughter's school to find ways of overcoming her little girl's fear of making mistakes. With a few tweaks to family life, and some persistence, you can see your children change and grow in their seven Cs.

Chapter 7

A call to action

The principal goal of education in schools should be creating men and women who are capable of doing new things, not simply repeating what other generations have done; men and women who are creative, inventive and discoverers, who can be critical and verify, and not accept everything they are offered.

Jean Piaget

Why do schools do what they do? If the case we are making for a different kind of school is so compelling, how come many more schools are not going down this route? The answer is that, although there is much rhetoric in England to the effect that schools have been given greater freedom, in reality, they have not.

In the following chart we have tried to give you a pictorial view of some of the forces which we believe influence what children in the UK learn today at school. We have identified how we view each of the seven different forces (parents/families, prominent and ordinary individuals, employers, charities, professional bodies, government) and

Parents and families by

- the school they choose
- the party they vote for
- their own individual actions to support schools

Prominent individuals via

- public statements and campaigns
- their influence on government/schools

Ordinary individuals via

- the party they vote for
- local statements and campaigns
- social media
- the practical actions they take

What schools actually decide to do

Government through

- the climate it creates for schools
- the national curriculum
- Ofsted
- its funding decisions
- the powers it gives local authorities

Employers through

- their public statements
- their influence on national/local government
- their actions to support or undermine schools

Charitable bodies by

- their public statements/campaigns
- their influence on government/schools
- the funding and support they provide

Professional bodies via

- their public statements/campaigns
- their influence on teachers
- their influence on government/schools

their alignment with the arguments we have made in the book so far.

Perhaps surprisingly, the employers align most closely with our views (as we saw in Chapter 5) and the government the least (although we acknowledge that, in this regard,

Scotland and Northern Ireland are more in agreement than England and Wales).

Various prominent individuals (some of whom we have met earlier), third sector groups (often charities) and professional bodies are leading the way. You might expect parents and families to be of the same mind. Surely they want the kinds of things that we are arguing for? The answer, we believe, is that they do. But they are cowed into going along with the status quo in the very understandable belief that there is not enough time to change things while their child is at school, so the best they can do is swallow their misgivings and go along with it. Even the excellent websites Mumsnet and Netmums have surprisingly little (yet!) to say about how parents can challenge the status quo. Mumsnet has thoughtful, supporting information about choosing schools and Netmums is full of great ideas for family learning, but neither grasps the mettle of our question:

What do you do if you are not happy with the way your child is being affected by school?

It was to provide an alternative vision that we decided to write this book, and in this chapter we suggest ways in which parents and teachers can take practical action.

But before you read on, we'd like you to stop and think for a moment about your own school days. Put aside for a moment any thoughts about how much you did or did not enjoy them (although that's clearly important) and reflect instead on how much they prepared you for whatever you are doing now.

You could do this as a private thought experiment in your own head, or if you feel more sociable you could try it out with your spouse, partner or a friend. Decide whether you are mainly recalling your primary school or thinking of when you were older.

1. What do you remember learning at school that is useful now?

2. What did you learn to *do* at school? (And can you still do it?)

3. What did you learn to *know* at school? (And can you still remember it?)

4. What did you learn to *be* at school? Or if this isn't clear, how about this: to what extent do you think your school shaped you as a person, your character? What was it that your school did which, with the benefit of hindsight, shaped your development? Was it for better or worse?

5. What is the most useless thing you learned at school?

6. What was the most useful thing you learned at school?

7. What would be on your national curriculum for children today? You could perhaps choose the age range of one of your children if you are a parent. Or if this question seems too technical, how about rephrasing it: what would you want an educated 11–19-year-old to know, to be and to be able to do? Or more fundamentally: how close would your ideal curriculum be to the kinds of suggestions we made in Chapters 1–4?

8. What other question would you like to ask about your own school days that might help you think more about schools today?

You may turn over your paper now (sorry if this brings back unhappy memories of classroom tests!). If nothing else we hope that these questions may have got you in the mood to think about schools today. In fact, here are two more questions to bring our list up to a round 10.

9. If you have a child or grandchild at school now, what do you like about your child's school and what would you like to change?

10. Thinking about schools more generally (especially if you were not able to answer question 9 as you're not a parent), from what you know about schools today, what do you like and what would you like to change?

For the purpose of this chapter, we are going to assume that you are a teacher, parent, grandparent or, at the very least, someone who is actively concerned in more than just a general way about the state of schools. We appreciate that if your concerns centre in particular on your own child's school, then you may feel conflicted. At worst, you might be afraid that if you start making waves at school it might disadvantage your child because the teachers will somehow be cross with you. Or worse still, you might imagine the teachers somehow taking it out on the parent (or child) who dares to challenge the school. We empathise. But we also want to encourage you to be bold.

Provided you start from the premise that you'd simply like to make your child's school even better in any way that you can, you are likely to be welcomed. Teachers are human and just walking in with your ten ways to fix this school may not be received in the way you intended. How you do what you do is going to be important. But unless teachers, parents and concerned adults *do* take action (along with employers, charities and others) we can't see how things are going to change in schools. In all of our experience – between us we have worked with thousands of schools – we have never found a school which was not delighted to meet with a parent who genuinely wanted to help. So how do you help?

There are three levels at which you might choose to act. The first one we explored in the previous chapter: working on your own 'domestic curriculum' at home. The second involves starting a conversation with your local school about how they might be even more effective at helping your child get ready for life. And the third involves tackling politicians and the wider bureaucracy of schools.

Before you talk to your local school, you might find this formula useful in planning your campaign.

$$D \times V \times F > R$$

It was dreamt up by a man called David Gleicher, who was trying to explain the three different elements which need to be in place if you are trying to overcome resistance to change. Here's what each letter means:

D = Dissatisfaction with how things are now

V = Vision of what is possible

F = First concrete steps that can be taken towards the vision

R = Resistance to change

If we were to try to summarise Gleicher's formula in words it might go like this: to overcome people's innate resistance to doing things differently you have to do three things. First, you have to explain really clearly what the problem is (if it ain't broke, why fix it?). Second, you have to make a pitch for a very different way of doing things, to get your listener to imagine a different scenario. And third, very quickly after you have done the big picture thing, you have to come down to earth and make two or three really practical suggestions as to how ordinary, fair-minded people could put your ideas into practice.

Let's assume for a moment that your local school is resistant to change. Take a moment to try this out in your own head or with a partner/spouse or fellow parent. Think of a school you know. What's wrong with it? Can you put your finger on your dissatisfaction? (I don't like the way … I really wish they wouldn't … It makes no sense in the modern world to spend time on … etc.) Don't worry if your language is emotional. That's why this is just a thought experiment or rehearsal at this stage!

Then have a go at describing your ideal school. (Imagine a school where … What I'd really like all children to learn is … In my view schools need to be different in these ways …) And, depending on what you have come up with, think of three or four simple and practical things you could suggest to bring about the kinds of changes you have in mind. Now you're good to go!

Helping your local school to change

Essentially, you need to shift the conversation away from the things that schools often want to talk about (subjects, attendance, uniform, tests, exams, options, etc.) towards the seven Cs, the development of your child's character, real-world learning and all the things which engage you as a parent. It will be helpful if, early on, you stress your commitment to the conventional indicators of school success, such as high grades in all subjects. (What parent or family member does not want the best possible grades for their child in whatever educational system they find themselves?) But at the same time you may like to say something like, "Naturally I want the best possible results for X, but I care passionately about how s/he gets the results. I also want him/her to develop ..." (add in the sorts of characteristics you want to see your child develop). Once you have started to have these different conversations, various opportunities will present themselves to you. You might be asked to:

- Share your ideas with other parents.

- Share your ideas with teachers.

- Talk to the head teacher or his/her senior staff.

- Talk to a class or assembly.

- Join a working group to develop thinking for the school.

- Become a parent rep promoting parental engagement.

- Run an after-school club.

- Help on a school trip.

- Contribute to a class project.

- Join the governing body as a parent-governor.

Of course, the school may be threatened by what you are saying and ask you to do none of the above, in which case you will need to be more persistent!

There are two useful ways of thinking about dealing with schools that may help you. The first is to think of the life stages of a child at school and all of the key transition points these offer you (choosing a nursery, starting at primary, moving on to secondary, choosing a college or university). At each of these new beginnings, you and your child have a one-off chance to ask some probing questions and, because the people you are talking to are likely to want to be a school of choice, they are likely to be at their most receptive.

Questions you might like to ask include:

- How does the school encourage children to develop a growth mindset? (See page 92 for more on this.)

- How does the school reward the efforts of its pupils?

- How does the school develop (choose any one of the seven Cs)?

- As well as the subjects on the national curriculum, which you will be teaching my son/daughter, what else will s/he be learning?

- What habits of mind are you trying to develop in children/young people at this school?

- What do you want children to be able to do when they leave your school?

- How do you involve parents at the school?

- How is the school preparing children for the real world?

Once in a school, you can use the rhythms of the school day/week/year (drop-offs and pick-ups, school concerts/plays/trips, parent–teacher meetings, PTA meetings) to ask about the kinds of things we have been thinking through. Every meeting with a teacher is a chance to ask about how your child is progressing as a person and as a learner, as well as finding out their attainment grades.

Parent–teacher meetings

For most parents, a parent–teacher meeting to discuss your child's progress will offer you an immediate opportunity to shift the conversation towards your child's happiness and emerging character, rather than merely listening to descriptions of her progress, typically in terms of attainment and effort. You could turn a "Ruby has only made a small amount of progress in her maths this term" into "I've noticed that Ruby seems to be much less interested in maths this term. Do you have any idea why this might be?" Or if the teacher is keen to talk about the test score or level of Ruby's achievement, but you notice that Ruby has been given a good grade for her effort, you might choose to 'ignore' the teacher's test grade and instead tell him or her how pleased you are to see that Ruby is trying hard in her maths.

In general terms, it is easier to shift the conversation on to a broader agenda if you start by noticing effort first and attainment second. If you can show you are interested in how your child goes about her learning, you are likely to have much more informative conversations with her teacher. And when you feel confident enough with some of the ideas in this book, you can start to suggest ways in which you might personally be prepared to help and support the school.

Get into the lobby and use your voice

The last of our three areas assumes that you are wearing your concerned citizen hat. It requires you to use the skills and tactics of a lobbyist. We start with some traditional methods and then suggest a few which are more recent. Remember, education (along with health, the economy and, from time to time depending on what is going on in the world, immigration) is something which voters always say they care about and which, therefore, politicians pay attention to. Before you lobby anyone you will need to work out what you want to say. If you have read the book up to this point and if you have tried the thought experiments, especially the ones at the beginning of this chapter, you will already be limbered up.

Tactics which are generally effective include:

- Describing what's wrong.

- Celebrating what's good.

- Making practical suggestions as to how things can be improved.

- Taking a line on a particular issue of the day.

- Comparing England (or whichever country you are living in) favourably or unfavourably with others elsewhere in the world.

- Quoting the views of business.

- Quoting the views of parents.

- Quoting the views of respected academics.

- Quoting the views of the older generation.

- Quoting the views of children.

None of these suggestions are mutually exclusive. Using a blend of them you could write to your MP, your local councillor, your local paper or a national paper.

If you want to be more targeted, you could write to the secretary of state for education or a minister responsible for an aspect of education (a quick google of 'Department for Education' will get you names and contact information). Or you could share your thoughts with the person who runs any one of the nine public bodies connected with education in England (currently Ofqual, Ofsted, Education Funding Agency, National College for Teaching and Leadership, Standards and Testing Agency, Office of the Children's Commissioner, School Teachers' Review Body, Social Mobility and Child Poverty Commission, and the Office of the Schools Adjudicator). Again, a quick web search will find you the contact details for these bodies. (There is no point in us including current details as one of the features of English educational decision-making is that names and roles keep changing.)

From this list you may only have heard of Ofsted. This is because (a) it's the most powerful, (b) it has a powerful press agency to share its views, (c) it makes a real difference to the lives of teachers and pupils, both for good and ill, and (d) the individuals who become Her Majesty's Chief Inspector of Schools tend to be people of strong opinions who like these to be heard widely. Unfortunately, some of the incumbents in the recent past have preferred proclaiming to thinking.

In the great scheme of things one letter is unlikely to change anything. But, increasingly, public bodies are required to analyse the correspondence they receive and publish information about customer/voter opinions (see also the details on Freedom of Information Requests below). So it may not be a complete waste of time.

If you prefer to talk to people rather than write, then you could start with your family and friends. The questions at the start of this chapter might help you to break the ice (I've been thinking about schools today, and remembering my own school days, and find myself wondering … Are you happy with your child's school? As an employer, how well do you think schools are doing these days?). This kind of lobbying is much gentler and more like a conversation. It can take place almost anywhere – over supper, in the park, at work, on a bus.

If you wanted to be more formal you could seek a meeting with some influential people. You might like to start with your local councillor, though remember that, in most parts of England, the councillor may not have direct powers over education. Nevertheless, he or she can pass views on to officers who do have responsibility.

And it is always informative to talk directly to young people about their experience of school. Once they are sure you are not going to nag them about their grades or their homework, or deliver the familiar little homily about how much their grades matter, they may be quite forthcoming. Almost always their views are perceptive, accurate and fair-minded, and will inform and enrich your own.

Two other options are also available. The first is a Freedom of Information (FOI) request. The Freedom of

Information Act (2000) gives you the right to access recorded information held by public sector organisations of the kind we listed earlier. Anyone can request information – there are no restrictions on your age, nationality or where you live. An organisation can refuse your request if the information is sensitive or the costs are too high, but most see it as their duty to answer such requests. Obvious targets for this kind of request at the national level are the Department for Education and Ofsted. Here are some examples of information which has recently been asked for and supplied:

- Cost of converting Liverpool College into an academy.

- Cost of administering SATs in primary school (SATs are the national tests).

- Number of school visits made by Michael Gove since January 2013 (Michael Gove was secretary of state for education between 2010 and 2014).

- Information about the number of children who had work experience at the Department for Education.

- Leave of absence: children missing school during term time.[1]

In each of these examples it is easy to see what the questioner is trying to get at. Questions asking about amounts of money spent or numbers of times something has happened work well. Or they can be framed as a more general request for information.

---

1 See http://www.gov.uk/government/
publications?keywords=&publication_filter_option=foi-releases&topics%
5B%5D=all&departments%5B%5D=departm
ent-for-education&world_
locations%5B%5D=all&direction=before&date=2012-11-01.

In terms of the arguments in this book you might like to ask about:

- The number of schools teaching resilience.

- The number of schools teaching thinking.

- Information about real-world learning.

- Information about 21st century habits of mind.

- Amount of time parents spend helping schools.

- Average cost of a child's education between 5 and 19.

To get a meaningful answer you might have to be more precise than we have been. But the point of an FOI request is not simply to get an answer but also to get a line of questioning onto the national agenda as the answers are published on various government websites.

The second specific lobbying option is an e-petition. According to the government's e-petition website, "e-petitions are an easy, personal way for you to influence government and Parliament in the UK. You can create an e-petition about anything that the government is responsible for and if it gets at least 100,000 signatures, it will be considered for debate in the House of Commons."[2]

At the time of writing, a petition to 'Reverse ban on holidays during school term time' is on the front page of the site. In a reasonable attempt to send a message about the importance of attending school, a ban on taking holidays in term time was introduced. But it has had various unintended consequences. Parents with very sick children have been prosecuted, as have parents wanting to take their family to spend time with a dying relative. The ban also poses a

2 See http://epetitions.direct.gov.uk/.

question that is close to the argument of this book: what is it about school that is so sacrosanct that a well-planned trip of a lifetime might not actually be full of more real learning than a few days of school? Could it be that the ban is more about our current obsession with Ofsted, as 'unauthorised absences' count against a school in its Ofsted report? Or are schools so geared to the taking of tests and examinations that they cannot think of a creative way to enable a pupil to carry on learning while on a holiday? Bill took his older son on an extended trip to Tasmania during one January term and the powerful learning experiences are still with his family more than a decade on. What teacher can honestly say that this would be true of a month of attending their lessons?

E-petitions cover many subjects. Here's another educational one currently struggling to get enough supporters: 'Much needed change to the rules in school with regards to head lice and nits'. It's tempting to make light of it, but any parent whose child has got nits from her school for the third time in a week will have considerable sympathy with the need for tougher enforcement of nit-free heads on children! (Interestingly the term 'nit-wit' comes from this unfortunate consequence of putting children together in a schoolroom!) If you go to www.educatingruby.org you can find out more about e-petitions relevant to our attempt to create popular groundswell to rethink schools. We will be suggesting an e-petition every half term until we create enough of a groundswell to change schools.

Using the web and social media

One of the simplest ways of finding out more and joining the debate about schools and education is to start to find your way around the growing number of educational blog sites. Many are written by thoughtful teachers or parents. Some are clearly mad. Many seem to believe that the answer to everything is technology. Most are deeply opinionated (aren't we all?). The best combine evidence, analysis of issues and description of promising practices in the way that we have attempted to do in this book. A good way of starting out here is to use one of the many 'intermediary sites' which signpost education blogs. You can do this by searching for 'best education blogs', for example. Ten years ago one enterprising company with great prescience even set up an annual award for the best education blog.[3] And you can vary your search technique to narrow the field as you wish – for example, 'most worthwhile education blogs' or 'UK education blogs'. On the website which accompanies this book (www.educatingruby.org) we have linked to bloggers who seem to us to be thoughtfully exploring the kinds of issues with which we are grappling.

Online videos are a useful source of ideas and a good way of entering into the debate. Set Google's search capability to 'Google Videos' and you can find much stimulating material, often through the medium of YouTube and increasingly using the TED talks format (powerful talks of less than 18 minutes' duration).[4] In the last few years, TED talks about education have been increasingly popular, with Sir Ken Robinson's RSA Animate talk, 'Changing

---

3   See http://edublogawards.com/.
4   See www.ted.com/.

education paradigms', challenging the educational status quo and arguing for the power of the arts, being viewed well over 13 million times.[5] Other thoughtful recent contributors include Sugata Mitra on how children's learning can be hindered by adults and enabled by the web and Jamie Oliver on the need for a food revolution in schools.

The web is full of both useful and distracting websites about the topics we are exploring in this book. Take any of our seven Cs for example – confidence, curiosity, collaboration, communication, creativity, commitment, craftsmanship – and play about with combinations of search strategies such as, 'how to develop confident children', 'how schools can develop children's curiosity', 'creative activities for parents and children', 'how to develop craftsmanship in children'. One of our favourite examples is 'Austin's Butterfly', which we have already mentioned. Turn on a few pages and we have included some more suggestions like this to get you started.

We shouldn't forget the ubiquitous Wikipedia in equipping you to enter the debate. While you will naturally need to apply appropriate caution to its claims, it is a prime example of collaborative learning in action. There is a growing educational movement which is at your fingertips via a search engine, starting simply with searches such as, 'educational wikis', 'educational wikis for parents' and progressing in whatever direction you want.

---

5 See http://www.ted.com/talks/
   ken_robinson_changing_education_paradigms.

There are various existing campaigns and grass-roots movements which may offer you encouragement and stimulate your thinking. These include:

● www.savechildhood.net – Save Childhood 'aims to identify and highlight those areas of most concern, to protect children from inappropriate developmental and cultural pressures and to fight for their natural developmental rights'.

● www.toomuchtoosoon.org – Too Much Too Soon believe that "children in England are starting formal learning too early, that the value of their creative and expressive play is being undermined, and that they are subject to developmentally inappropriate pressures that are damaging to their long-term health and wellbeing".

● www.unicef.org.uk – The work of UNICEF UK is based on the UN Convention on the Rights of the Child, which sets out the rights of every child, no matter who they are or where they live, to grow up safe, happy and healthy.[6]

● http://en.unesco.org – UNESCO regularly contributes to research and practical action to promote well-being in children and young people.[7]

These are just four examples. There are many more from which you might derive good ideas.

---

6 See, for example, UNICEF, Child well-being in rich countries: a comparative overview. Report card 11 (2013). Available at: http://www.unicef.org.uk/Images/Campaigns/Report%20card%20briefing2b.pdf .

7 See, for example, Asher Ben-Arieh, Measuring and monitoring the well-being of young children around the world. Background paper prepared for the Education for All Global Monitoring Report 2007. Strong foundations: early childhood care and education. Available at: http://unesdoc.unesco.org/images/0014/001474/147444e.pdf.

Running in parallel with the web are the various social media options. Probably the most relevant here is Twitter. There are people who tweet about policy, research and class-room practice. Tweets can, of course, be utterly banal, but increasingly thoughtful tweeters are using them as a means of signposting more substantive resources on the web. The discipline of the 140 characters allowed in a tweet can also be a useful clarifying and focusing device! On this book's website – www.educatingruby.org – we have a Twitter feed (something that we have only very lately started) as well as links to those we think are contributing to the education debate we want to see. As with everything we have been suggesting in the last few pages, searching for 'best education tweeters' and so on will narrow the field.

If your exploration of blogs, websites, videos and wikis begins to become overwhelming, one simple self-protection strategy is to set up a Google Alert with a small number of key words in it. It will then prompt you by email when a chosen blogger has made a new post or something new has appeared on a particular topic. If you want to further screen out content then try Google Scholar which will take you to sites which start from a research context.

The simplest thing you can do is to join the debate on www.educatingruby.org. In doing so we can begin to see how many of us share a common view of what needs to change in schools. At a practical level you can also find out which other parents, grandparents and concerned citizens are active in your local area and join forces.

Finale

Let us finish by reminding you why your voice and your participation are so important. The changes that need to happen involve encouraging, connecting and celebrating the initiatives of the kind we illustrated in Chapter 5. There are many, but they are still in the minority. If we are to reach the tipping point that is needed, they have to scale up faster. In terms of Gleicher's formula, we have to help people to artic-ulate their dissatisfactions with the status quo, to be able to imagine a better future and to understand the small, practi-cal steps that can help any school make progress firmly in the right direction. All of these are vital because resistance is still high in many places. Change takes energy, so people need reassurance and encouragement – and a bit of pres-sure – to put in the effort it takes. We need to keep reassuring everyone that the results go up, not down, if you do start to shift the school's culture.

If change is to happen faster, though, we need not just brave school leaders but a change in the political weather. General elections are a competitive event that come round every four or so years. They are like the World Cup, but with only a small number of teams. Politicians' lives are geared around these events, and the worst thing that can happen is to lose. The very worst thing that can happen for any indi-vidual politician is to do something that contributes to their side losing. This means that, for much of this five-year cycle, politicians are obliged to play defensively, at the same time as creating the impression of doing all kinds of things that are eye-catching and important. They have to look busy and decisive, while at the same time doing nothing that might upset the *Daily Mail* or the Murdoch press. This all means

that they cannot engage with anything that is subtle, complicated, hard to sell or long term. In other words, they are
condemned, by the very nature of short-term, cyclical, competitive, two or three party politics, to fail to do what is
necessary – especially as far as education is concerned.
Politicians are bound to do too little, too late. It's a miserable
position to be in, and they deserve our sympathy.

Unless. Unless the mood of the populace changes, and
they begin to fear that they will lose substantial numbers of
votes if they don't do what is required. Only the real fear of
losing is strong enough to force them to overcome their natural caution. Only when it looked like the No Campaign
might lose the Scottish referendum was the Westminster
bubble galvanised into action. Only when UKIP threaten to
drain substantial numbers of voters from the Conservative
Party does the leadership respond – first by bullying and
then, if that doesn't work, by shifting policies to try to attract
those perfidious voters back.

At the moment, the best chance of getting our educational movement heading in the right direction is for all of
us to get off our backsides, stirring up our friends and rela-
tions, asking awkward questions of our MPs, signing online
petitions, fighting for places on the governing bodies of our
local schools and all the rest of it.

It's not about party politics; it's about how to get people
in power to do the right thing. It's about being able to speak
confidently about our dissatisfactions: the amount of time
wasting and real damage that too many schools still inflict on
bright young minds. It's about being able to talk passionately
about the need, and the practicality, of focusing more
intently and explicitly on the development of 21st century
character strengths. It's about sharing as widely and loudly
as we can the stories of deep success that we come across

– not just crowing about A level results. If we can do that, policies will begin to change, the political wind will begin to fill the sails of change and teachers will feel support for finally being able to teach in the way that made them want to do the job in the first place. They will be truly able – as our friend Art Costa has put it – to prepare young people not just for a life of tests, but for the tests of life. And that will make millions of young people, and their families, very happy.

Thirty ways you could help a local school[1]

In many cases the offer of help (even if refused!) can stimulate thought on the part of the school and, once you have started you will never look back as you develop a more meaningful relationship with the school. You are likely to be asked to undergo a DBS (Disclosure and Barring Service) check (which used to be called a CRB or Criminal Records Bureau check) to ensure that you are a suitable person to be working with children.

1. Share your enjoyment of a hobby with a class or after-school group.

2. Offer to run a school club.

3. Offer your time and talents – computing, gardening, engineering, painting.

4. Offer to talk about life in a different country.

5. Offer to coach a small group of students in reading, maths, languages, computing, art or any other subject in which you are confident enough to help.

6. Help coach a team.

7. Offer to help with or start a music group.

---

1   This list draws heavily on the list created by the Center for School Change at http://www.ncrel.org/sdrs/areas/issues/envrnmnt/ famncomm/pa1lk20.htm. You can augment it by searching for 'ways parents can help schools'.

8. Help children put out a school or classroom newsletter.

9. Volunteer to help on a school trip.

10. Help create a display.

11. Help build something such as a storage area for work in progress or a tree house.

12. Volunteer to answer the schools' phone.

13. Demonstrate cooking from a particular country or culture to students.

14. Help bring senior citizens to school to watch a student production.

15. Share information about your workplace or chosen career.

16. Help arrange learning opportunities in the community such as an internship or apprenticeship for a student at your business, organisation or agency.

17. Host a one-day 'shadow study' for one student, or a small group of students, about your career in business or some other organisation.

18. Go on a local field trip with a teacher and a group of students.

19. Help to create a natural area outside the building where students can learn.

20. Join the PTA and increasingly play an organising role.

21. Help design a parent and/or student survey for the school.

22. Help arrange for a political leader (mayor, city councillor, MP) to visit the school.

23. Help write a proposal that would bring new resources to the school.

24. Donate books or materials to the school.

25. Help other parents develop their parenting skills.

26. Help organise a workshop for parents on ways they can help their children to learn.

27. Help write, publish and distribute a list of parenting tips.

28. Start a parents' reading group or Twitter book group (see pages 199–201 for book ideas).

29. Start an Educating Ruby group www.educatingruby. org at school (you can print off posters and find lots of templates to use in your school and local area).

30. Create your own list of 30 ways to help your school!

A selection of thought-provoking books

The following are just a few books that have made us think, including some of our own:

Baumeister, Roy and Tierney, John (2012). *Willpower: Rediscovering Our Greatest Strength* (New York: Penguin).

Benn, Melissa (2012). *School Wars: The Battle for Britain's Education* (London: Verso Books).

Carner, Lauren and Ladavaia-Cox, Angela (2012). *Raising Caring, Capable Kids with Habits of Mind* (Mechanicsburg, PA: Institute of Habits of Mind).

Claxton, Guy (2008). *What's the Point of School? Rediscovering the Heart of Education* (Oxford: Oneworld Publications).

Claxton, Guy, Chambers, Maryl, Powell, Graham and Lucas, Bill (2011). *The Learning Powered School: Pioneering 21st Century Education* (Bristol: TLO).

Claxton, Guy and Lucas, Bill (2004). *The Creative Thinking Plan: How to Generate Ideas and Solve Problems in Your Work and Life* (London: BBC Books).

Dweck, Carol (2006). *Mindset: The New Psychology of Success* (New York: Random House).

Gardner, Howard (2009). *Five Minds for the Future* (Boston, MA: Harvard Business School Press).

Gatto, John Taylor (2002). *Dumbing Down: The Hidden Curriculum of Compulsory Schooling* (Gabriola Island, BC: New Society Publishers).

Gerver, Richard (2010). *Creating Tomorrow's Schools Today: Education – Our Children – Their Futures* (London: Continuum).

Hallgarten, Joe (2000). *Parents Exist, OK?* (London: Institute for Public Policy Research).

Henderson, Ann, Mapp, Karen, Johnson, Vivian and Davies, Don (2007). *Beyond the Bake Sale: The Essential Guide to Family-School Partnerships* (New York: New Press).

Kaufman, Gershen (1999). *Stick Up for Yourself: Every Kid's Guide to Personal Power and Self-Esteem* (Minneapolis, MN: Free Spirit Publishing).

Kaufman, Scott Barry (2013). *Ungifted: Intelligence Redefined* (New York: Basic Books).

Layard, Richard and Dunn, Judy (2009). *A Good Childhood: Searching for Values in a Competitive Age* (London: Penguin).

Lucas, Bill (2006). *Happy Families: How to Make One, How to Keep One* (Harlow: BBC Active).

Lucas, Bill, Claxton, Guy and Spencer, Ellen (2013). *Expansive Education: Teaching Learners for the Real World* (Melbourne: Australian Council for Educational Research).

Palmer, Sue (2007). *Toxic Childhood: How the Modern World Is Damaging Our Children and What We Can Do About It* (London: Orion).

Perkins, David (2010). *Making Learning Whole: How Seven Principles of Teaching Can Transform Education* (San Francisco, CA: Jossey-Bass).

Robinson, Ken and Aronica, Lou (2010). *The Element: How Finding Your Passion Changes Everything* (London: Penguin).

Rosen, Michael (2014). *Good Ideas: How To Be Your Child's (and Your Own) Best Teacher* (London: John Murray).

Simister, C. J. (2009). *The Bright Stuff: Playful Ways to Nurture Your Child's Extraordinary Mind* (Harlow: Pearson Education).

Tough, Paul (2013). *How Children Succeed: Grit, Curiosity and the Hidden Power of Character* (London: Random House).

Waters, Mick (2013). *Thinking Allowed on Schooling* (Carmarthen: Independent Thinking Press).

Willingham, Daniel (2012). *When Can You Trust the Experts? How to Tell Good Science from Bad in Education* (San Francisco, CA: Jossey-Bass).

About the authors

I'm Guy. I'm 67, and I don't have any children of my own. I like most children and enjoy their company, but I worry about whether school is giving them the best possible preparation not just for further study but for life. I went to a primary school in North London. The headmaster (as they invariably were in those days) was a stern man (at least to a 5-year-old) called Mr Giles. I was so worried about making mistakes in my exercise book that I rubbed right through the paper and had to go to the head and be told off. Sewing made me really anxious – my grubby child's hands sweated so profusely that they turned the cloth into a dirty rag. Mr Giles again. I went back there a couple of years ago to look around. They still had the register from 1953 and there I was! The current head was Mr Herring. He was much nicer. I found they are now using an educational approach my colleagues and I have developed called Building Learning Power (BLP). How things have changed.

When I was $8\frac{1}{2}$ we moved to the West Midlands, and between the ages of 9 and 18 I went to King's School Worcester. I had the potential to be a chorister, but my mum thought it would interfere with my lessons. She was educationally ambitious for me. Mum was a piano teacher and dad was a clerk in the Midland Bank (now HSBC). I did unexpectedly well at O level (the forerunners of GCSEs), and as a result consciously decided that 'being bright' was an option, so I studied harder and got into Cambridge. Before going to university, I taught chemistry for a few months and discovered a bent for explaining tricky things in engaging ways, which has never left me.

But Cambridge chemistry went too fast for me to understand properly so I got dispirited, my results plummeted and I switched (much to mum's dismay) to psychology, which I took to like a duck to water. I found you could argue and theorise about evidence and not just remember it. I went on to get married and do a doctorate in psychology at Oxford. In August 1973 my marriage broke down and my doctorate was failed. I discovered that my reserves of resilience and resourcefulness were massively unequal to the emotional turmoil I was experiencing. Out of this, with the help of a great counsellor, I evolved a lifelong interest in the personal side of learning, and have spent the rest of my life researching and writing about it. (I eventually gained my doctorate, and got very happily remarried, so all's well that ends well!) In recent years, with the help of Bill and a host of adventurous colleagues and teachers, I have been designing small, smart, practical things that teachers can do that develop pupils' confidence, independence and pleasure in wrestling with difficult things – and get better results in the process. That's what Building Learning Power is.

* * *

And I'm Bill. My dad was a teacher. He became headmaster of a school called King's School in Gloucester and then an HMI – one of Her Majesty's Inspectors of Schools. On a day soon after he became an HMI he proudly told my sister and me that he was going to be the eyes and ears of the Queen in schools and help them all to become better. So education has always been a big thing in my family – though a mixed blessing. I remember resolving at the age of 19 that the one career I would have nothing to do with was teaching! Four years later I found myself standing in front of a group of 12-year-olds about to explain the mysteries of English tenses to them – and discovered I loved teaching. I trained as a teacher, taught in some tough schools, and by the late 1980s I was a deputy head teacher in a large secondary school in West London, and Kenneth (now Lord) Baker (remember him?) was set on introducing something called the national curriculum. I decided that I'd take a sideways move and went to Winchester to set up a new charity called Learning through Landscapes, and then came back to London to be chief executive of the Campaign for Learning. In 2008, with Guy, I created the Centre for Real-World Learning at the University of Winchester.

I've got three children, 10-year-old twins (a boy and a girl) and an older son, who is 23. School didn't seem to inspire my eldest son as much as he had hoped and consequently I don't think his school days were the happiest of his life. I think he really found something that stimulated him when on an internship year as part of his university degree. My younger two have their ups and downs but are hungry to learn new things and often do seem to be stimulated by their current school. Things they do out of the classroom – sport, music, church and Cubs – are at least as important to them as lessons. Current passions are birds of prey, singing, rollerblading, ice hockey, piano and loom bands (a craze that may have been forgotten by the time you read this!).

These days, often in collaboration with Guy, I spend my time trying to puzzle out, from the perspective of a parent, researcher and ex-school leader, how we can make schools better places. Oh, I forgot to tell you. I'm 59, so I've got nearly a decade to go before I catch up with my co-author!